D00915.25

AN INTRODUCTION TO
THE TEACHING OF WRITING

WITHDRAWN

Stafford Library
Columbia College
1001 Rogers Street
Columbia, Missouri 65216

D0910930

AN INTRODUCTION TO THE TEACHING OF WRITING

STEPHEN N. JUDY
Michigan State University

SUSAN J. JUDY
Central Michigan University

JOHN WILEY & SONS
New York   Chichester   Brisbane   Toronto

Copyright © 1981, by John Wiley & Sons, Inc.

All rights reserved. Published simultaneously in Canada.

Reproduction or translation of any part of
this work beyond that permitted by Sections
107 and 108 of the 1976 United States Copyright
Act without the permission of the copyright
owner is unlawful. Requests for permission
or further information should be addressed to
the Permissions Department, John Wiley & Sons.

Library of Congress Cataloging in Publication Data:

Judy, Stephen N.
An introduction to the teaching of writing.

Bibliography: p.
Includes index.
1. English language—Composition and exercises—
Study and teaching. 2. English language—Rhetoric
—Study and teaching. I. Judy, Susan J., joint
author. II. Title.

PE1404.J82   808'.042'07073   80-25163
ISBN 0-471-06222-7

Printed in the United States of America

10 9 8 7 6 5 4 3 2 1

ACKNOWLEDGMENTS

As part of our research for this book, we wrote to a number of friends and colleagues around the country asking them to supply us with writing curriculum "artifacts"—course syllabi, lists of objectives, program designs. We have drawn on this material extensively to develop our sense of the current state of composition teaching in American schools and colleges and to provide specific examples of programs currently in operation. For their assistance we are grateful to Teddi Baer, Bellvue, Washington, Public Schools; Anita Brostoff, Carnegie-Mellon University, Pittsburgh; Candy Carter, Placer County, California, Public Schools; Mary K. Croft, University of Wisconsin at Stevens Point; James Davis, Grant Wood Area Educational Agency, Cedar Rapids, Iowa; Alan Dittmer, University of Nebraska, Lincoln; Marjorie Farmer, Philadelphia Public Schools; Michael Flanigan, Indiana University, Bloomington; Richard Gebhardt, Findlay College, Findlay, Ohio; Jeff Golub, Kent, Washington, Public Schools; Toni Haring-Smith, University of Illinois, Champaign-Urbana; William Horst, Henrico County, Virginia, Schools; Betsy B. Kaufman, Queens College, Flushing, New York; Jay Lalley, Loyola Academy, Wilmette, Illinois; Barrett J. Mandell, Rutgers University, New Brunswick, New Jersey; Jack McGarvey, Bedford Junior High School, Westport, Connecticut; Frank McTeague, Borough of York, Ontario, Canada; Beatrice Morton, Bowling Green State University, Bowling Green, Ohio; John Osheka, Classical Academy, Pittsburgh, Pennsylvania; Jesse Perry, San Diego, California, City Schools; Patricia Phelan, Hale Junior High School, San Diego, California; Frank Ratliffe, Gunn High School, Palo Alto, California; and Harriet Stolorow, Jackson, Michigan, Community College.

The material on evaluation in Chapter 8 was enriched by the proceedings of a Conference on Evaluation conducted at Michigan State University: E. Fred Carlisle, Chair, Department of English; Jay B. Ludwig, Director of Writing; Principal Consultants: Richard L. Larson, City College of New York; Lee Odell, State University of New York at Albany; and Joseph Domenic, National Institute of Education, Washington.

Stephen N. Judy
Susan J. Judy

CONTENTS

INTRODUCTION

TEACHING WRITING: CHALLENGE AND OPPORTUNITY

The good news/bad news joke has become standard in the repertoire of many comedians. The good news is often deceptive, less good than it might appear superficially. The bad news is usually terrible.

COMEDIAN: I've got some good news and some bad news.

AUDIENCE: What's the good news?

COMEDIAN: The good news is that this summer you'll be able to buy all the gasoline you want, with no shortages.

AUDIENCE: (Cheers. Then . . .) What's the bad news?

COMEDIAN: The bad news is that you'll have to drive to Saudi Arabia to pick it up.

There is good news and bad news about the teaching of writing, but it is no laughing matter.

The good news is that at no time in the history of education have more people been interested in the teaching of writing. Composition has been a cover story for several national magazines; it has been discussed on TV talk shows right along with popular topics like dieting and personal psychology; it comes up in cocktail party conversations and in parent—teacher conferences; it dominates interest at professional gatherings of English teachers.

The bad news that lurks beneath is that many of the people expressing concern are badly informed about the writing problem. Often they know little of the nature of language acquisition or about ways and means of teaching writing. Thus the demands being made on composition teachers are often retrogressive and contradictory, leaving the writing teacher wondering just what sort of action to take.

While a comedian should never have to explain a joke, we want to elaborate on our view of the news, both the good and the bad.

We think it is generally good news that interest in writing is high, because for too long writing has been a kind of stepchild within the curriculum. At the college level, for example, English departments have argued that the teaching of writing is beneath them. As early as 1890, a committee reviewing the teaching of composition at Harvard College stated:

> It is obviously absurd that the College—the institution of higher education—should be called upon to turn aside from its proper functions, and devote its means and the time of its instructors to the task of imparting elementary instruction which should be given even in ordinary grammar schools, much more in these academic institutions [the college preparatory schools] intended to prepare select youth for a university course. (Adams, 1902)*

Few people would disagree that colleges should not have to do "elementary" or "grammar school" work, but in this statement, an attitude of distaste—almost repugnance—toward teaching writing is evident. That attitude has persisted in many colleges and universities to this day. The teaching of writing, particularly a basic course such as freshman composition, has been taken as an onerous chore, and departments have sought ways of eliminating it from the curriculum.

However, the lower schools have not been any more eager to take up writing instruction. Junior and senior high school teachers are by and large more interested in literature than in composition, and this interest is shown in the amount of time they devote to writing. In a major study done in the 1960s, James Squire and Roger Applebee (1968) discovered that in selected "exemplary" high schools, only 15.7 percent of instructional time was given to composition, and much of that time was devoted to theme correction instead of actual composing experiences. Even with the present interest in composition, we doubt that the figure would be much higher today. Literary study continues to dominate the secondary school curriculum.

In the elementary grades, teachers have generally been more interested in spelling and penmanship than in original composition, so much so that when one uses the word "writing" around elementary teachers, most of them assume that one means "handwriting."

It is good news that the current public and professional awareness of the importance of writing seems to be changing attitudes at all levels—even if gradually. Some colleges have begun taking basic writing courses more seriously, seeing them as an opportunity to serve students, not simply as a burden. Secondary school teachers have signed up for writing workshops and institutes in large numbers, and, as evidenced by articles in professional journals, these teachers are experimenting broadly with writing instruction in their classes. Elementary teachers, too, have shown signs of learning that writing involves more than copying, and they are discovering the great creative power that even their youngest writers have.

But the news is obviously not as good as it might seem, for the interest in writing has arrived accompanied by harsh, often destructive criticism of

* Complete references for cited works will be found in the Bibliography.

teachers. *Newsweek* (1975) accused English teachers of creating a generation of "semiliterates"; parents grumble about what they perceive as the incompetence of laziness of teachers; college and high school students complain (as they always have) that no one has taught them how to write. Even within the profession teachers have launched attacks on one another, usually with those at the upper levels having a better vantage point to lob critical shots at those at the lower:

> *It's time to gripe again!*
> *It's high time to ask what high schools are doing in their English classes to prepare students for anything like a college class. On the basis of the students I see in my freshman classes I would have to say that most of the high schools are doing very little.* (Ledbetter, 1974 p.50)

Of course, thoughtful criticism and self-evaluation have an important place in the educational system. However, it is clear that much of the current criticism is not well directed. Nor does it always come from people who might reasonably be considered authorities. Teachers and professors of English have long known that just about everyone believes himself or herself to be an expert on the teaching of English. People will remain silent in the presence of a science or math teacher—someone who commands a factual body of information—yet most have no hesitation at all about telling English teachers how to do their jobs. Too often these "outsiders" and nonspecialists feel free to describe what ought to be done in the schools and colleges, and often their advice is bad, based on a sentimental view of their own school experiences and the way things were done in the "good old days."

Even when criticism has been presented by professionals, it has not always been based on an unbiased view of the writing problem. Too seldom have critics from within the profession made a careful study of the issues and problems involved before presenting their assessments. Note, for example, the biases that emerge in this discussion from *Empty Pages* by Clifton Fadiman and James Howard (1979), a report on writing instruction sponsored by the Council for Basic Education:

> *We are not about to become a nation of total illiterates. Nor on the other hand will any nostrum cure us. The patient will neither expire nor spring from bed like a son of morning.*
> *But there is a bed and in it lies a patient. Let the cloudy term* trouble *describe the illness. We are all in some sort of trouble, most thoughtful readers will agree, over the teaching and learning of writing. What sort of trouble? How much trouble? What kinds of teaching and learning? What kinds of writing? Who is ailing? Should the patient be helped? Or should we merely remain observant, diagnosing the condition as a normal part of the birth trauma accompanying the appearance of a new type of human being—a nonliterate citizen in a fully technological culture?* (pp. 9–10)

We consider ourselves to be as "thoughtful" as most readers, and we do not think that everything is as it should be with the teaching of writing; yet we find ourselves unwilling to accept the Fadiman/Howard view of the "trouble." They have chosen an ancient, clichéd metaphor for their discussion: that of the student as diseased patient, the teacher, by implication, as doctor. By selecting that metaphor and extending it, they have presented a pessimistic, even fatalistic, view of the student as learner. Fadiman and Howard have become aloof and even arrogant; they sound like two physicians impersonally debating whether or not to prolong the life of a terminally ill patient.[1]

Given that metaphor, it does not surprise one to find elsewhere in the book the statement that the "elements of competent writing" begin with "penmanship and spelling," move to "grammar" and "other elements" (including commas and the paragraph), next focus on "idiom, usage, correctness," then dwell on "precision," and only last take in "thinking and organization." Virtually any contemporary linguist or composition theorist will explain that Fadiman and Howard have their order exactly reversed: that idea and content in writing must precede surface correctness. Further, there is considerable research to show that dwelling on the elements of correctness does little to bring about positive changes in students' writing.

But Fadiman and Howard are not knowledgeable about this research. In fact, they take an antiacademic stand in describing themselves and the members of the commission they represent:

> We . . . have in common the advantage that we are not "experts" in the field of "compositional theory," but working teachers, writers, and editors. (p. 1)

While one has to respect that practical experience, it is apparent that experience unaccompanied by rational, critical thought is not especially valid as a form of learning. The net effect of Howard's and Fadiman's order of priorities is to tell thousands and thousands of teachers to begin teaching at the wrong place, to resurrect teaching methods stressing the elements of surface correctness that were properly discarded generations ago. Fadiman and Howard are part of the bad news.[2]

---

[1] Lest our interpretation seem extreme, we want to point out that at about the same time Fadiman was quoted recommending that a book attacking current language standards should be read before "we all become illiterate." It is Fadiman, not we, who is prone to exaggeration.

[2] Nor are these two writers the only ones of their kind. Along with their book we list as bad news *The Literacy Hoax* by Paul Coppelman (Morrow, 1979), *What's Happening to American English?* by A. M. and Charlene Tibbetts (Scribner's, 1979), *Less Than Words Can Say* by Richard Mitchell (Little, Brown, 1979), and *Paradigms Lost: Reflections on Literacy and Its Decline* by John Simon (Clarkson N. Potter, 1980).

At this point it is appropriate for us to introduce a metaphor of our own, that of the young writer as *seed* or *new plant*. We admit that our metaphor is just as clichéd as the one used by Fadiman and Howard, but ours has the advantage of being in keeping with the considerable body of linguistic, compositional, and rhetorical research that exists. (We are writers, teachers, and editors, too, but unlike Fadiman and Howard, we take pride in being composition theorists as well.)

The seed or plant metaphor suggests that every human being has an intrinsic capacity for language growth and development. We see this capacity in our baby, Michael, who, at this writing, is six months old and struggles—physically—to make signs, gestures, and noises that will communicate. We see it in a group of elementary school children with whom we recently worked in a neighborhood theater project where they designed, wrote, produced, and televised a series of one-act plays. We see it in the hundreds of high school students who turn out for young writers' workshops and who are delighted to publish their writing in anything from mimeographed broadsheets to slick school magazines. We see it in college freshmen who come into basic writing courses nervous and intimidated and who leave feeling confident and in control of their writing. We see it in teachers enrolled in graduate writing workshops who, for the first time in years, turn their pens to writing and discover the joys of writing and teaching others to write.

Extending the seed metaphor, we see the writing teacher, not as a doctor, but as a gardener: one who readies the soil, keeps down the weeds, and helps the plants grow to their full potential. Of course, a gardener must worry about some plant diseases, but most gardeners agree that the best defense against plant ailments is to grow strong plants in the first place. Further, there are natural, organic ways of controlling garden diseases and pests; one need not douse the entire garden in poisons just to save a few ailing specimens.

Like any metaphor, the seed/plant one cannot be extended too far. For instance, there is an implication of predestination in comparing writers to seeds: When you plant a seed, you know precisely the kind of plant you will get, how tall it should become, the kind of flower or vegetable it will yield. Working in the writing garden does not give such predictable results. Because the human imagination is not restricted, one never knows precisely what kind of "crop" it will produce. But that mystery is part of the pleasure that emerges from teaching writing: Students, and thus their teachers, can be infinitely imaginative.

If one shares our positive attitude toward students' potential for language, in general, and writing, in particular, the "trouble" with writing looks a lot different. Johnny and Jane certainly don't write as well as they should, but they are not terminal cases either. We don't think they are even sick. If there is a crisis, it is not that disease is rampant; it is, rather, that too many seeds do not fall on plowed ground where they can be cultivated successfully. Too few students of all ages come across the vital element that will help them grow: an informed, concerned, imaginative, industrious, dedicated teacher of writing.

At the risk of pushing our metaphor too far, we want to observe that the current educational climate is one in which teachers of writing and writing programs can flourish. The bad news presents a challenge; the good news offers an opportunity. If teachers take the good news—that people are concerned about writing—at face value and do not concern themselves too closely with the bad news—the misguided advice that is offered so freely—they can build programs successfully. This book suggests some ways and means.

We invite the reader to join us in attempting to make the good news better.

CHAPTER 1

THE BASICS OF TEACHING WRITING

The effect of the Russian launching of Sputnik on American education is legendary. When, in 1957, the Soviets were able to put their satellite into orbit ahead of a rival United States project, it was generally accepted that Russian technology, and, by implication, Russian education, was superior to our own. No level of schooling and no academic discipline escaped the angry criticism that emerged when Americans discovered their educational/technological system was no longer Number One.

In retrospect, we can see that much of the criticism was unfair. For one thing, the Russians had put together a crash program that had left other areas neglected.(Americans would, of course, engage in their own crash program to put men on the moon and thus regain the lead in the space race. That program, in turn, would create technological and economic deficits elsewhere.) Even more important, it is now apparent that the schools could not be given all the credit, in the Russian case, and all the blame, in our own. Many diverse social, political, and economic conditions and factors were responsible for the technical achievement of putting a basketball-sized chunk of metal into earth orbit.

Still, Sputnik catalyzed what had been growing dissatisfaction with American schools, including criticism of the original Johnny and his reading skills (Flesch, 1966). Critics argued that the schools had "gone soft," that progressive education had weakened the curriculum and taken out all the substance. They worried over the then considerable interest in education as social adjustment. After Sputnik, most Americans felt it was time to put some rigor back into the schools.

The federal government responded to this public criticism by funding a series of education projects. Initially, the concern was for mathematics and science education, the hard disciplines that would help to create a new, superior technology. With the support of federal monies, subject specialists and educators created "new" curricula based on the assumption that the deepest, most fundamental understandings of the disciplines could be presented to young people in comprehensible fashion (Bruner, 1960). The new math was developed; new curricula in physics, chemistry, and biology emerged; and these programs were quickly accepted in the schools.

Literacy education was not included in the first round of federally sponsored reforms. But under intense lobbying from the National Council of Teachers of English (1961), reading and writing were included in an expanded Congressional bill that carried the telling label, "National Defense Education Act." "Project English" centers were established at universities across the country, and these centers began to examine school and college English and to determine how and why it was failing. The centers were to create a new theoretical base for English and to prepare programs that would teach this "new" English successfully. The critical self-examination that followed led to research, exploration, and growth in all areas of English, including our central concern in this book: the teaching of writing. The effects—the shock waves—of both Sputnik and the new English can still be felt today, over two decades later.

In this chapter we will first review the changes that have taken place in writing theory and instruction over those twenty plus years. Then we will sketch out what we believe to be the principal points of agreement among theorists and practitioners in composition and rhetoric, showing the consensus among members of the profession. Finally, we will briefly discuss a few of the many areas of debate that remain in composition teaching today.

The first phase of the post-Sputnik revolution centered on reviewing what was called "the tradition" in writing instruction. This tradition has deep roots that can be traced as far back as medieval teaching of Latin, but for practical purposes the tradition began in the nineteenth century with the grammars of people like Lindley Murray (1795) and the rhetorics of Alexander Bain (1869) and others. The approach emphasized mastery of the principles of sentence structure (grammar) and the organization of longer units of discourse (rhetoric), with emphasis on what can be called "the complete thought method." Textbooks began by instructing students in the nature of the sentence, defined as "a complete thought": first parts of speech; then the whole sentence; finally sentence varieties—simple, compound, complex. Next students were taught the paragraph, also defined as a complete thought, with a topic sentence stating the thought, several more sentences developing it, and a final sentence concluding or summarizing it. Third in the instructional hierarchy was the whole composition, itself a complete thought with introduction (in which the main idea was stated), body (in which the idea was developed), and the conclusion (which summed up the thought). Whole compositions were categorized into discourse forms, usually four: *narration, description, argumentation,* and *exposition,* each with its own stylistic and rhetorical characteristics. The traditional approach is probably familiar to many readers of this book, since it persists in many handbooks commonly used in schools and colleges.

The new English investigators of the 1960s, however, found little that was satisfactory in this nineteenth century tradition. Modern essays, they discovered, seldom conform to the rigid structure of the essay as described in the handbooks. The validity of the four forms of discourse was questioned: *Narration,* for example, seldom appears apart from *description; exposition* and *argumentation* blend into one another. Nor did the four forms explain or describe such mixed types of writing as the personal essay. In general, the tradition seemed too concerned with teaching students about the nature of writing—albeit not very accurately—while offering little writing practice.

Most damning to the tradition, however, were studies that investigated the relationship between knowledge of grammar and actual composition skills. Although many research studies had been conducted since the beginning of the century, none had shown any significant correlation between mastery of parts-of-speech grammar and writing ability. (For a summary of these studies, see Haynes, 1978.) Traditional grammar was further discredited for its fundamental inaccuracy; it had been based on Latin grammar models that had little correspondence with English syntax (Sledd, 1959).

Into the vacuum created by dissatisfaction with the tradition came what were called the "new grammars," first, *structural* grammar based on analysis of word classes (Sledd, 1959) and, soon after, *transformational generative* grammar, concerned with methods of sentence construction (Chomsky, 1964). The new grammars quickly found their way into textbooks, most notably the school and college texts of Paul Roberts (1958, 1967).

New rhetorics followed shortly. Francis Christensen of the University of Nebraska broke the ice with a series of articles describing his "generative" rhetoric of the sentence and the paragraph (1966). Soon the issues of professional journals—particularly *College Composition and Communication*— were filled with arguments and counterarguments on aspects of his system as well as with proposals for alternative rhetorical schemes. Some theorists, led by Edward P. J. Corbett, then of Creighton University, argued that no new rhetoric was needed at all, that the classical rhetoric of Aristotle and his followers was sufficient to describe modern writing (1971).

The era of Project English and the new English pretty well spanned the decade of the 1960s; it was a period of ferment, discussion, and debate. In the end, no single new English was identified or agreed on by a majority of writing teachers. In fact, within classrooms, the traditional approach continued to dominate and it is still probably the single most widely used approach today). However, the critical discussions of the 1960s forced teachers to acknowledge the weaknesses in their composition instruction and to begin searching for new ways of teaching writing.

The Project English centers were not the only places where the teaching of composition was being discussed. In the mid-1960s a group of teacher/ writers often called the "romantic critics of education" voiced their concern—their anger—about the state of education, including writing. John Holt (1964), Jonathan Kozol (1967), Herbert Kohl (1967), Edward Herndon (1971), and others wrote devastating attacks on what they saw as the regimentation and joylessness of the public schools (and the colleges as well). In direct contrast to the new English reformers, they felt that there was too much rigor and content emphasis in the schools, too little concern for the personal development and individual freedom of children. Their approach to writing involved no rhetoric or grammar instruction at all. Instead, they revelled in letting students enjoy "free" writing experiences, where ideas flowed first and form and content were worried about later, if at all. The writing of these critics was itself vibrant, enthusiastic, and compelling, and thousands of teachers all over the country began to adopt their techniques.

Within the ranks of English teachers beliefs parallel to those of the romantic critics were also evolving. At a British and American seminar on the teaching of English held at Dartmouth College in 1966, study groups examined a number of issues and problems, including evaluation of the new English and its emphasis on content and structure. Many seminar participants favored an approach that deemphasized grammar and rhetoric to focus on the student's personal growth through language. The title of the central seminar report, John Dixon's *Growth Through English* (1967), suggests the consensus. The Dartmouth Seminar put an end to enchantment with new grammars and rhetorics and set off another round of exploration and debate. Such writers as Ken Macrorie (1970), James E. Miller, Jr. (1972), and Peter Elbow (1973) argued that imagination, idea, and thinking were at the heart of the writing process. Miller summarized the arguments against the traditional, form-centered approach in his composition textbook, *Word, Self, Reality*:

> [This is not] a book about externals of form—sentences, paragraphs, essays; exposition, narration, description, argumentation; fiction, poetry, drama. All of us have rudimentary notions of these elements or forms. And laboring over elaborate definitions among them will contribute little to our writing. . . . What this book does attempt to do is to restore awareness of the mystery of language and respect for its ways and possibilities. . . . (p. 3)

Where the central issue of the 1960s had been a debate over the content of the writing course—Which of the new grammars and rhetorics shall I teach?—the debate of the 1970s was one of form versus process: Do I teach writing structure at all, or do I allow the imagination to provide the flow and structure of words on paper? The debate generated many side issues as well: Did one teach principally practical writing such as the essay and the research paper, or was it more appropriate to let students explore imaginative, creative writing? Did one correct usage errors on papers or was it more important to allow students to speak and write their own natural ways?

Such complex questions were engaging the profession deeply when the back-to-basics "crisis" broke in the mid-1970s. Triggered by reports of standardized test score declines, back-to-basics essentially rejected *all* the new pedagogy. The new math, which had been highly praised a decade earlier, was ridiculed for allegedly failing to teach students to add, subtract, and multiply. The new science, many claimed, was not teaching enough facts and basic concepts. The new English, whether modern grammar, new rhetoric, or freewriting, was rejected as having contributed to illiteracy among children.

As had been the case a decade and a half earlier with Sputnik, most of the complaints came from the general public through the media, and there was clearly a serious lack of confidence in teachers' abilities. When taxpayers and commentators called for back-to-basics, they meant a return to the educational practices of their youth, a return to pre-Sputnik instruction in grammar, paragraph practice, and essay writing.

The initial response of most writing teachers to this outcry was, quite naturally, defensive. There was no clearcut evidence that new methodology could be blamed for the test score declines. Indeed, given the diversity of school curricula, it seemed that the traditional instruction that had persisted in the schools might well be at fault (Gillis, 1967). These murky waters were darkened further by reports showing that the standardized tests that had led to the uproar—most notably the SAT—could not reliably be used to assess individual student achievement accurately, much less employed to gauge the state of the educational system (College Entrance Examination Board, 1977; Nairn and Nader, 1980).

However, as the 1970s drew to a close, writing teachers began to take more positive action, launching new school and college writing programs in response to public demand and meeting with their critics to clarify points of disagreement. Thus it seems quite possible that the decade of the 1980s will be one of consolidation, in which the various, often conflicting theories and practices of the 1960s and 1970s are reviewed, discussed, and, as possible, consolidated in well-founded writing programs.

Though many conflicts remain (and not all of them can be resolved), at the present time the profession seems to have reached broad agreement on many of the essentials of good writing programs. In the remainder of this chapter we will present our view of the nature of that agreement.

SOME POINTS OF AGREEMENT ON THE TEACHING OF WRITING

WRITING IS A LIBERAL ART. On one point, at least, virtually everyone—the public, students, teachers, liberals, conservatives, progressives, traditionalists—seems to be agreed: Writing is a skill that is central, not only to education, but to all of life. With the exception of the related skill of reading, no school learning is drawn on more often in school and after graduation than writing.

Although some people have argued that writing has become obsolete in our media-oriented world, writing remains fundamental, even as electronic communications media become more important. For instance, even though people can now dial direct by long distance anyplace in the world, they still keep scratch pads and pencil stubs by the phone. Even though the development of home computer and word processing systems has provided electronic means of information storage that do not require pen and paper, those same systems have encouraged a broad spectrum of people to learn and master new composing skills: computer keyboarding and writing in computer languages. Even though television-based and computerized instructional systems are becoming more common, the schools and colleges continue to depend on writing—notetaking, paper writing, exam writing—to a high degree. The day may have passed when people spent their leisure hours keeping detailed private journals and writing long discursive letters (did the majority of people ever do that, we wonder?), yet writing seems to us not to have seriously diminished in importance. There will always be a need for people to be able to use language skillfully, to write with clarity and ease.

We agree with Edwin Newman (1974, 1976) when he says there is a need to improve the precision with which people use language (although we find his linguistic purism unwarranted). There is too much gobbledeygook and doubletalk afloat in the world; there are too many obfuscating memos and instruction manuals; there is too much writing that is aimed at deceiving, rather than presenting the truth accurately. Good writing programs are needed to help young people and adults write clearly, forcefully, directly, and honestly. This need will not diminish, even in the face of new and more efficient electronic devices, whether picturephones, wrist radios, voice transcribers, memory-bank typewriters, or science fiction gizmos not yet imaginable.

But writing is more than a practical skill, more than a tool for accurate, clear communication. The post-Sputnik years have led to research showing that writing contributes broadly to the learning process.

One of the most serious limitations of the traditional approach is that it regards writing as a kind of "clothing" for ideas. One takes "thoughts," which presumably exist well formed in the brain and "dresses" them in language for display. Thus most of the conventional handbooks place a great deal of emphasis on the elements of writing "fashion," creating rules for writing—for "dressing"—that are independent of actual content: "Vary your sentence structure." "Never use a long word where a short word will do." "Don't use first person pronouns when writing an essay." In actual practice, such advice is often quite worthless for the novice because it fails to take into account the substance of the writing.

Sentence variety, for example, grows naturally from content that is rich and complex instead of shallow and superficial. The variety or length of sentences is not something that inexperienced writers can manipulate arbitrarily without losing control of their own voice and style. Similarly, the handbook advice about word choice seldom works out in practice because words and ideas are not separable. One cannot deliberately select a short word, a near-synonym, when a longer word is precisely what is needed; nor can one reverse the process and pick polysyllabic Latinate words when a good, one-syllable Anglo-Saxon word will do. Finally, advice on pronoun choice often is unhelpful because the choice must reflect point of view, the audience for whom one is writing, the style one wants to affect, and so on.

Of course, experienced writers experiment with and manipulate some of these surface features for stylistic effect, and their practices may, on occasion, reinforce the handbook rules. But in general, the effect of the writing-as-clothing approach is to create writers whose sense of structure and style is inappropriate. Most often one sees it in student writing that is strained, stuffy, or hyper-correct: "In the opinion of this writer it is my conclusion . . . "

Writing is more than dressing up ideas by putting them in language. Writing, we believe, is a liberal art—it functions as a source of self-discovery as well as of learning.

For example, writing allows a person to make a record of events and emotions for the purpose of discovering their significance. Poetry, as Wordsworth said, is emotion recollected "in tranquility," allowing the writer to reconsider it, capturing its significance. Essay writing can also be a process of discovery, and numerous writers have attested to the fact that they don't fully understand their beliefs until they have argued them on paper. Even the writing of a short story can be a process of self-discovery for a writer, who projects ideas, situations, experiences—some fictional, some slight variations on his or her own experience—and who thus provides opportunity for introspection.

"Know thyself" is an aim of classical education, and teachers from the Greeks and Romans to the present time have recognized the role writing plays in realizing that aim. When people write, they go through a figurative and literal soul searching, synthesizing ideas and composing them for public inspection. There is a strong element of truth in the schoolroom cliché: "Unless you can write it, you don't understand it." The cliché applies to the understanding of self as well as to knowledge of things and events outside the self.

Thus writing is a means of learning, often an act of discovery. Most of us have had the experience of realizing, right in the midst of composition, that we have discovered something new, that we are off writing on a tangent that we had not intended to explore. While such moments are too rare, they help to reemphasize the point that writing is not just dressing up thoughts. It is inextricably bound up with the *making* of ideas.

Discovery through writing is exhilarating, even joyful, which points to another area neglected by the traditional approach: the intrinsic satisfaction and pleasure involved in writing. Finishing off a well-written piece and presenting it to an audience that is responsive can be very satisfying. It carries with it a sense of achievement and an appreciation of community. Writing need not be just an onerous task of transcribing thoughts to paper. Because it is creative, because it involves human communication and interaction, it should be a pleasurable, personally valuable activity.

Writing pleasurable? Joyful? To many adults it is not, and they are astonished that it could be to some. But we observe with interest that in school the youngest children find no particular anxiety in writing. They do not get writers' blocks. If one asks for a story, a first grader will make one up on the spot, using whatever crude penmanship skills he or she has developed. It appears that as people grow older and move into higher levels of schooling, writing is used more and more frequently as a testing medium, and in the process, fear and distrust of writing begin to build up.

This is not to suggest that all writing anxiety is school-induced. Certainly many fears about writing are created by the adult realization that one's writing is judged in an all-too-competitive world. But it is important to recall that in its natural state—during those early years of childhood language acquisition—writing does not seem to be any more threatening than speaking.

Nor are adults altogether excluded from the pleasures of writing. One need merely glance at a monthly issue of *The Writer* magazine to get a sense of the existence of a community of writing-lovers, people pursuing careers as writers, mostly for fun, occasionally for profit. One sees these people at public poetry readings, and their numbers are reflected in the submissions to national writing contests and festivals. Millions of adults *like* to write.

Further, a person does not need to write in the so-called creative forms or write for pay to find satisfaction. There is pleasure in compiling a good research report, a good memo to the boss, a good speech, a good love letter. It is unfortunate that so many college and school writing courses have been joyless affairs.

Writing courses have often had the stamp "service course" on them. The comp course was a place where one mastered language skills that would be practiced elsewhere—in the "real" world, in "real" subject-matter courses. The comp course had no real life of its own. "If we didn't need your 'services'—your grammar and your footnote methods," teachers have been told tacitly, "we wouldn't need your course in the curriculum at all." For composition teachers to recognize that writing is a means of self-discovery, that it is a way of learning, that it can be a pleasurable activity, may have helped to legitimize composition courses and given writing teachers a sense of their own worth.

We believe that even if all students could write competent prose, even if they could spell every word correctly and could identify every noun and verb with 100 percent accuracy, there would still be a need for instruction in writing for students of all ages. One never stops learning about oneself and the world; one can never get too good at shaping ideas and beliefs through writing; one never outgrows the joy of writing.

But for composition courses to merit their position in the curriculum, programs must provide a broader range of writing experiences than they have in the past. A writing program needs to provide students with time and opportunity to explore private thoughts through language. It must offer diverse ways of writing about experience: plays, poems, and stories as well as essays. It should be based on the knowledge that writing involves discovery, that in a writing course students learn, not just about English, but about life—about themselves, other people, science and technology, literature and art, politics . . . about whatever interests or concerns or delights or appalls them. Such a program has a practical dimension that prepares students for real world tasks by recognizing that writing is *the* liberal art.

WRITING IS TAUGHT AS A PROCESS.   As new rhetorics competed with old during the early 1960s, each attempting to do a better job of enumerating and naming the parts of English composition than the others, another alternative to the traditional approach to writing was emerging. Professor Wallace Douglas of Northwestern University stated it as a "proposition" (1966a), but in the years that followed, it became a *fiat:*

Composition is a process, and what ought to be taught in a composition class is the operations, in their order, that make up the process of composition. (p. 184)

Douglas and other theorists held that the traditional approach had failed (and the new rhetorics would likely fail) because they treated composition teaching as a matter of presenting for mastery the forms or structures of language. The students learned grammar and rhetoric (new or old) and tested out their skill at matching accepted forms.

The advocates of writing-as-process felt that instead of learning terminology, students needed to learn—and, more important, to experience—the steps and stages involved in writing itself: planning, drafting, revising. If students could master these fundamental processes, it was argued, they could apply those skills in a variety of writing situations.

Perceiving writing as process led to other fascinating questions: What *is* this process? What are its parts or components? How does the process differ from one discourse mode to another? Does it vary from one writer to another? Such questions were investigated in studies that ranged from reminiscences by individual writers about how they learned to write (Watkins and Knight, 1964; Amberg, 1977) to formal research into the composing habits of young people (Emig, 1971). Investigation of the writing process is continuing today. Understandably, research has not produced a fixed or rigid model of the composing process. It has, nevertheless, suggested that the process can be discussed in three major phases:

Prewriting—perceiving the world, discussing ideas, focusing on the needs of an audience, taking notes, gathering resources, and planning the paper.
Writing—the actual act of composing.
Postwriting—revising, editing, preparing final copy, copyediting or proofreading, receiving the response and criticism of readers.

The process varies considerably from one writer to another. Some people find it necessary to spend a very long time on the prewriting stages, mulling over a paper and its details until they have a plan firmly in mind. Others take the "rough" in rough draft literally and plow ahead with writing, letting details and structure work themselves out as the paper is written.

Writers even develop highly idiosyncratic mechanical procedures that, for them, may become inseparable from the process of composing itself:

Robert Frost worked at a writing board—never a desk. Occasionally he would jot lines on his shoe.
Jacqueline Susann produced five drafts of each of her novels, each draft

on different color of typing paper. First drafts were on yellow, followed by blue, pink, and cheap white paper.

The fifth and final version was typed on very expensive white stationery "To impress my publisher."

Raymond Chandler typed his novels on half-sheets of yellow paper to reduce the amount of retyping when he made mistakes. (Felton and Fowler, 1980)

Yet even while there has been recognition of the idiosyncratic nature of the writing process, there has simultaneously (and regrettably) been an impulse in some teachers to try to regiment it. Instead of letting the various parts of the process flow into one another, with each writer following her or his own particular style, some teachers march classes through the process step-by-step: "First it's prewriting. Everybody done? Now write. Finished? Now revise." There is even a book on "strategies" for teaching individual stages of the process in isolation from actual writing assignments (Koch and Brazil, 1978). In that book such skills as "discovering form in writing," "building bigger sentences," and "learning punctuation conventions" are taught just as they were under the conventional approach. The process of writing becomes reduced to yet another set of exercises and drills.

The moral ought to be clear: In perceiving writing as a process, composition theorists recognize that it is fluid, individualistic. Though common elements can be identified for all writers (each of us *organizes*, for example, one way or another), the process cannot be segmented into tiny particles, with each one taught separately and monitored by every writer.

Perhaps the most exciting and challenging implication of the process view is that writing teachers must think of their students as individuals, not as a uniform group of twenty-five or thirty writing machines. No two students will tackle a given writing problem in precisely the same way: no two will use the same techniques of planning; no two will write identical outlines or notes; no two will perceive the audience the same way; and assuredly, no two will begin or end at precisely the same time or put the same words on paper. The diversity built into a writing-as-process approach challenges the teacher to individualize the writing class. Further, it leads to a tough question that gets directly to the heart of this book: How the devil does one teach this elusive process of composing?

WRITING IS A LEARN-BY-DOING SKILL. To us, the great body of research and informed speculation about writing (not to mention the common sense and collected experience of generations of teachers) points directly to the conclusion that writing is learned through experience; that is, writing is learned by writing. One learns to shape ideas on paper by struggling to get them down; one learns what will please audiences by trying to please them; one learns the ins and outs of style by writing and by rewriting sentences. Composing is a learn-by-doing skill.

John Dewey was the pioneer in articulating the learn-by-doing approach, or, to be more precise, in describing the ways in which experience *is* education. But writers and educators have long known—or at least sensed—that mastery of the language comes through practice, not study of language forms. Here is the statement of a high school teacher written over eighty years ago, just *before* Dewey's time:

> *Language is acquired only by absorption and contact with an environment in which language is in perpetual use. Utterly futile is the attempt to give a child or youth language by making him learn something about language. No language is learned except as it performs the function of all speech—to convey thought—and this thought must be welcome, interesting, and clear. There is no time in the high school course when language will be learned in any other way.* (Thurber, 1898)

The writer, Samuel Thurber of Girls' High School in Boston, was addressing himself principally to spoken language, but he believed that the hypothesis was true for writing as well.

A phrase like "learn by doing" is, in itself, simplistic and subject to multiple interpretations. A skeptic, for instance, might reasonably ask, "If writing is a learn-by-doing skill, why don't children learn it outside of school?" Or, more bluntly, "If writing is learned by doing, who needs writing teachers?"

In fact, a surprising number of people *do* learn writing outside of school without the help of teachers. Just ask them. It is not at all uncommon for a writer—professional, hobbyist, or business person—to say, "I never did learn to write in school. What I know, I learned on the job." We place ourselves in that group, having mastered what we know of both writing and the teaching of writing through firsthand experience, not principally through school or college courses.

At the same time, we do not advocate deschooling society or abolishing writing courses to leave students free to pick up knowledge on the streets. At least ideally, schools are useful, even vital places for students to gain experience—including writing experience—in systematic ways. The schools also provide a good forum for students to think about experience—including writing—critically and carefully. Though it is possible to learn on the streets, the beauty of a good school is that it makes learning easier, more comprehensive, and more substantial.

An important implication of the learn-by-doing philosophy is that the principal task of the teacher is *not* to tell students about language forms or structures or to show them ways in which they write badly (or even well). It is not to run them through the grammar book, the spelling book, the vocabulary workbook, or the rhetorical handbook. The task is to create an environment in which students can engage their minds and pencils in the writing process: gathering materials; thinking about structures and plans; drafting, editing, revising; sharing their work with an audience.

The long and short of it is that the writing program must provide for frequent writing. Our biggest criticism of both school and college writing instruction is that students simply don't do enough of what they came to learn: writing. Like jogging six miles, swimming fifty laps, or playing lead guitar, writing becomes easier if one does it regularly.

However, those readers who already have some experience teaching writing may want to raise an objection: Assigning quantities of writing seems almost impossible given current teaching loads, particularly in the secondary schools, but in many colleges as well. Teachers who must face 150 students five days a week (as is the case in far too many high schools) cannot assign and respond to very many themes. College freshman writing instructors who teach three sections with a total of ninety to one hundred students find it difficult to assign, collect, and evaluate as much as a single piece of writing from each student every week.

We acknowledge the difficulties imposed by those loads (we have faced them). And we have argued with both school and college administrators that if they want to improve their writing programs substantially, they need to reduce course loads for writing teachers. At the same time, we are not optimistic that in the immediate future those loads will be reduced. For the present, composition teachers will be facing an overload.

We are also convinced that even under less-than-ideal conditions, school and college teachers can increase the amount of writing they offer. Many teachers spend far too much time on peripheral study and drill, particularly grammar, spelling, and vocabulary, when the time could be better used by having students write. In addition, by "writing" we don't necessarily mean fully polished, thousand-word essays. We believe that writing teachers should make greater use of short, informal writings—notes and memos, letters, summaries, short reports, journals and so on. Writing should be used as a mainstream form of communication, not just brought into the curriculum on "theme writing Fridays" or used exclusively as a way of testing young people. Finally, we do not think English teachers should be the only ones who ask students to write; writing should be assigned and evaluated in every class in the school.

We suspect that the idea of a learn-by-doing approach with emphasis on the quantity of writing may sound *laissez faire* to some teachers, reminiscent of the legendary Summerhill where students learned at their own pace. Although we advocate independent, self-guided learning, we do not recommend a totally unstructured approach. We see learning by doing taking place in a carefully organized classroom, with a busy, informative, constructive teacher guiding the writing process. To clarify how learning takes place in this setting, it is useful to explore an additional point of general agreement within the profession, that centering on the reality of the writing experience given to novice writers.

WRITING EXPERIENCES MUST BE AUTHENTIC. In *Growth Through English*, the report of the Dartmouth Seminar, John Dixon (1967) wrote:

> *Language is learnt in operation, not by dummy runs. In English, pupils meet to share their encounters with life, and to do this effectively they move between dialogue and monologue—between talk, drama, and writing.* (pp. 6−7)

Dixon's comment about "dummy runs" ought to bring nods of agreement from writing teachers. Too much of what happens in writing classes is a "dummy run," with students practicing: combining short sentences into long ones, choosing the "right" word on multiple choice vocabulary worksheets, writing practice paragraphs to imaginary audiences.

In order for discovery learning—learning by doing—to take place, the writing experience must be authentic for the students, which means that they must see some intrinsic value to it. They should be able to use it to engage in some "encounters with life," to use Dixon's phrase. Exercises and drills obviously lack this authenticity, even when the material is made clever or turned into a game. Further, many writing topics commonly assigned fail to achieve authenticity because they do not engage students in matters that directly concern them.

Writing assignments need not be terribly intimate or glorify trivial experience to be authentic. Often students will draw on autobiographical material, but writing about current issues and affairs can also engage them. They can write animated pieces about literature, career interests, hopes and ambitions, problems around the school or college, or research. Nor do assignments necessarily have to require the writing of essays to take on authenticity; students of all levels can turn their ideas into poems, plays, stories, television scripts, journals, memoirs, and dozens of other forms.

The point is that a writing topic must make contact with the student, touching his or her life. A colleague of ours, Arthur Athanason of Michigan State University, explains that he tries to get students to write with *passion*—though not necessarily flaming passion. Only when their writing is passionate and intense does he feel he can help them develop as writers. To practice rhetoric or pedagogy on a passionless composition is a fruitless exercise, a "dummy run" for the *teacher*. As Athanason says, getting students to write with passion is not easy. From the time they enter school, most students are discouraged from making their writing intense; indeed, the dummy run exercises students experience in the schools are enough to drain their writing of life. Part of the challenge of teaching writing, then, becomes finding topics that will engage or even provoke students into writing authentic pieces.

An assignment alone cannot bring reality to the writing process. As Dixon says, "writing implies a message: the means must be associated with the end, as part of the same lesson." Writers need someone to read and respond to what they have written. Occasionally that someone will be a teacher—in Dixon's words, "A pupil turns to the teacher he trusts for confirmation of his own doubts and uncertainties in the validity of what he has said and written." For many students, however, presenting writing to a teacher is too closely associated with evaluation and criticism; the teacher is perceived as a theme grader instead of an adult who can be trusted. Writers need other readers as well—readers in the plural. Only as they begin to see how their writing affects others can writers learn by doing and improve their writing skills.

Most contemporary writing theorists are agreed that the end of the writing process should not be the teacher's comments or, worse, just a letter grade. Within the classroom, the audience can often be the students' peers, people who generally share common interests and tastes. But writing for audiences beyond the classroom is important, too, and we spend considerable time in our own courses trying to help students find other people for whom they can write. Though students can occasionally write successfully for imagined audiences—rhetorical projections, as it were—for the most part authenticity comes to the writing process when students can aim their writing at live bodies, people who will give them genuine response.

We are aware, as are most writing teachers, that even with good assignments and real audiences, the in-school writing process can never be made *totally* authentic. Teachers have to face the fact that many of their writing courses are not taken voluntarily by the students, and the interest of the students in learning to write may be minimal. In theory, truly authentic writing is self-motivated, growing from the writer's need to explore and communicate ideas, but in practice, writing grows from something called "the assignment," which the teacher imposes on the students, hoping it will be real to them. Similarly, although peers can serve successfully as an audience for student writing, the practice of passing papers around a classroom circle—good as it may be—is somewhat contrived, an approximation of writing in the real world.

At the same time, the very unreality of the school or college classroom offers the writing instructor some distinct advantages. For one thing, a classroom is a safer place to explore and experiment with writing ideas than is the real world. The environment of the writing class can be more accepting, more protective of the novice, than the tough atmosphere of "the street." Most important, the writing classroom provides an opportunity for the humane, skillful teacher to control, guide, and develop what is essentially a naturalistic process: learning to write.

To return to the gardening metaphor we developed in the Introduction, the classroom can serve as a greenhouse, an authentic but ideal place for beginning writers to develop their skills. Of course, there is the danger of creating hothouse plants; the teacher can be overly accepting or too generous with praise, thus making students unduly sensitive to outside criticism. But in our experience such a problem is relatively rare—those kinds of compositional orchids are seldom produced. If the greenhouse-keeper is skilled, he or she will be able to raise sturdy young plants that can be "hardened off" when the season is appropriate and placed in the natural garden, where, because of their favored upbringing, they can compete with wild plants more than successfully.

Our argument for authenticity in teaching writing thus resolves two apparently contrary principles: that students need to write authentic papers for real audiences, and that the writing classroom itself can never be completely authentic. Teachers can capitalize on the unreality of the classroom by making it more than real, a better-than-real place for students to write.

EVALUATION SHOULD BE GIVEN IN PROCESS.   Traditionally, the belief has been that students learn to write by having their errors on finished themes pointed out to them. However, the principles we have described in the previous two sections—writing as a learn-by-doing skill and the need for authenticity—suggest that, to the contrary, students learn writing skills most satisfactorily by solving writing problems, discovering what works and what doesn't work during the process of writing. This, in turn, suggests alternative approaches to evaluation of papers.

In our own classes, we try to make evaluation a constant part of writing, not just something done after the fact of composition. Students discuss and evaluate potential ideas before forming a plan or beginning to write; they test out sentences and paragraphs with one another and with the teacher as they write; they meet in small groups to discuss first and second drafts and possible revisions. We also try to involve ourselves in evaluation early. "Draw on our knowledge *while* you write," we tell them. "Don't surprise us with final copy we've never seen before. Let us help you along the way."

In-process evaluation is, we think, more authentic than *ex post facto* criticism. No writer that we know writes principally for the purpose of getting criticism of his or her writing, but most writers are eager to get help and advice along the way. Because this advice helps smooth the way toward a successful composition, it is more likely to be taken to heart than criticism administered later.

Some teachers question whether students can give one another helpful advice during the writing process. "It's the blind leading the blind," they claim. "Students don't know anything about writing and therefore can't help each other." Though it may be correct to say that most students know little of the formal aspects of writing—rhetoric, for example—we find that they are nonetheless able to give helpful, authentic responses to each other. They need help in learning how to react to papers, a topic we will take up in detail elsewhere. But they also have an advantage over the teacher because their response is generally presumed to be authentic by the writer. Students are sometimes tough—too tough—on one another, but their comments and criticism, even when not framed in the formal language of a teacher, seem valid and are thus perceived as useful.

THE POINTS OF AGREEMENT: IN SUMMARY

In this chapter we have developed five broad principles for writing courses and programs:

1. Writing is a liberal art.
2. Writing is taught as a process.
3. Writing is a learn-by-doing skill.
4. Writing experiences should be authentic.
5. Evaluation and criticism should be given in process.

These principles will serve as the philosophical center for the remaining chapters of the book; each one will be developed and amplified.

To support our assertion that the principles do, in fact, represent general points of agreement within the profession, we refer the reader to the accompanying chart on p. 24, "Standards for Basic Skills Writing Programs." The twelve statements were developed by a Committee on Writing Standards of the National Council of Teachers of English (NCTE) for use by teachers at all levels. Actually, the list is less a set of "standards" than a consensus view of what is important in the teaching of writing.

We also want to bring the reader's attention to a summary statement on the value of writing made by that same committee:

> *Beyond the pragmatic purpose of shaping messages to others, writing can be a means of self-discovery, of finding out what we believe, know, and cannot find words or circumstances to say to others. Writing can be a deeply personal act of shaping our perception of the world and our relationships to people and things in that world. Thus, writing serves both public and personal needs of students, and it warrants the full, generous, and continuing effort of all teachers.*

On that concluding sentence, too, most of those committed to teaching writing can agree.

STANDARDS FOR BASIC SKILLS WRITING PROGRAMS

An effective basic skills program in writing has the following characteristics:

TEACHING AND LEARNING

1. There is evidence that knowledge of current theory and research in writing has been sought and applied in developing the writing program.
2. Writing instruction is a substantial and clearly identified part of an integrated English language arts curriculum.
3. Writing is called for in other subject matters across the curriculum.
4. The subject matter of writing has its richest source in the students' personal, social, and academic interests and experiences.
5. Students write in many forms (e.g., essays, notes, summaries, poems, letters, stories, reports, scripts, journals).
6. Students write for a variety of audiences (e.g., self, classmates, the community, the teacher) to learn that approaches vary as audiences vary.
7. Students write for a wide range of purposes (e.g., to inform, to persuade, to express the self, to explore, to clarify thinking).
8. Class time is devoted to all aspects of the writing process: generating ideas, drafting, revising, and editing.
9. All students receive instruction in both (a) developing and expressing ideas and (b) using the conventions of edited American English.
10. Control of the conventions of edited American English (supporting skills such as spelling, handwriting, punctuation, and grammatical usage) is developed primarily during the writing process and secondarily through related exercises.
11. Students receive constructive responses—from the teacher and from others—at various stages in the writing process.
12. Evaluation of individual writing growth:
    (a) is based on complete pieces of writing;
    (b) reflects informed judgments, first, about clarity and content and then about conventions of spelling, mechanics, and usage;
    (c) includes regular responses to individual pieces of student writing as well as periodic assessment measuring growth over a period of time.

Source: Tate, 1979.

SOME PROBLEM AREAS AND POINTS OF *DIS*AGREEMENT

In presenting the NCTE statement and our own five points, we do not wish to imply that there is anything like complete unanimity among either composition theorists or practitioners. In the real world of teaching, people are arranged on a broad spectrum from those who agree with the principles completely to those who are convinced that the tradition never failed and that a return to basic grammar and rhetorical drill is warranted. We believe our position is clearly supported by contemporary research, but we think it would be unwise for us to end this chapter without sketching what we see as the major points of disagreement as well as some remaining serious problems in the teaching of writing.

THE ROLE OF DRILL.   We wholeheartedly support John Dixon's assertion that writing is learned in practice, not through dummy runs. At the same time, many people feel that *some* drill or exercise is useful, and those people apparently include the members of the NCTE writing standards committee. (See their statement #10.)

The enlightened argument in favor of drill acknowledges that such exercises as sentence diagramming are useless in teaching writing. However, proponents claim that limited drill, especially if based on linguistic or rhetorical principles, may be valid. Most prominent among the advocates of limited drill are those who recommend an exercise called "sentence-combining." (Mellon, 1969; O'Hare, 1973; Strong, 1976. For critical review of their research, see Marzano, 1976.) The sentence combiners use principles of transformational grammar that have students practice combining short kernal sentences into longer ones. This drill, the advocates say, consumes only a small portion of the time given to composition, and they have conducted research showing that the drill may carry over into student writing, at least for short periods.

The most commonly offered counterargument to sentence combining (and to most other enlightened kinds of drill) is that the concepts can usually be taught much more effectively during the writing process itself. We think the best sentences for students to combine (or, better, to edit) are their *own*, not exercise-book fabrications. Further, drill is drill, no matter whether its roots are in ancient grammar or contemporary linguistics. As the learn-by-doing philosophy states, students learn what they actually *do* in school. When they drill, they learn the drills; when they write, they learn to write.

We believe that virtually any concept or skill required by a writer— whether penmanship, usage, structure, organization, or style—is best taught through actual writing rather than through dummy runs. Thus we disagree with those who say that even modest amounts of drill are either necessary or useful.

THE TREATMENT OF MECHANICS AND USAGE. It is axiomatic in the profession to say that matters of correctness in writing are secondary in importance to content and ideas. (See the NCTE statement #12.) Yet we find that in practice the principle is often violated—that teachers concentrate on errors in mechanics and usage first and pay only lip service to content. Typically, teacher comment on content and ideas is brief and superficial, while notes on errors in mechanics and usage are described in vivid detail.

We do not advocate sending students into the real world or into subject-area classes with a vague notion that correctness doesn't matter or that "only ideas count." Every speaker and writer knows that surface correctness has definite effects on how an audience responds. But we also believe that content *does* precede correctness, and we vigorously object to the practices of teachers who use students' writing principally as a medium to teach mechanics and usage.

Further, we are convinced that when an authentic writing experience takes place, language change happens naturally, including matters of correctness. When students write for real audiences they naturally seek ways of getting their writing into appropriate form. No writer wants a passionate piece rejected simply because he or she failed to follow some accepted conventions. But it is inauthentic for teachers to claim they are concerned about a young person's ideas and opinions and then to act as if correct English were far more important. In the end, we think that a process approach can "handle" correctness by placing it in the context of whole writing experience, a point we will develop in subsequent chapters.

THE DEMEANING OF COMPOSITION AND ITS TEACHERS. Although interest in teaching writing has increased dramatically in the past two decades, the sad fact remains that teachers of writing are not well respected. Many colleges persist in seeing freshman writing as a necessary evil instead of an opportunity to teach, and high schools often give the new teachers a heavy composition load, a sure sign that the senior faculty doesn't want to teach writing.

There is no question in our minds that teaching literature is easier than teaching writing, if only because there are fewer papers to grade. However, it is equally clear to us that composition theory is just as complex and intellectually stimulating as literary criticism, and that teachers of literature should not consider themselves superior to those who teach writing. We support the idea of a balanced curriculum where literature and composition flow into one another and are afforded equal amounts of time in the curriculum and equal amounts of respect from colleagues.

TEACHING LOADS IN COMPOSITION. In one respect, at least, composition is not the equal of literature: It can't be taught effectively to large groups. The literature teacher may be able to handle thirty-five or more students in a class and still get the points across successfully. The writing teacher cannot do a good job with the same numbers, much less so if he or she is teaching three or four writing courses at a time. Yet, in most schools and colleges, composition is treated as an equal in terms of course assignments and responsibilities—one comp course equals one lit course; comp and lit courses are the same size. The writing teacher, we believe, deserves special consideration if he or she is to do an adequate job. We advocate reduced class size for courses that deal exclusively with writing and believe that no teacher should have to teach more than two composition courses at one time.

THE RESPONSIBILITY FOR TEACHING WRITING. As we have already implied, school and college faculties seem all too ready to isolate writing and make it the province of a few, overworked teachers. We believe that writing should be diffused throughout the entire English program by being made a part of literature courses and that it should be taught throughout the school by teachers of chemistry, physics, drivers ed, and geography, as well as English. At the present time, however, school and college faculties seem complacent about school-wide writing programs, and administrators do not appear willing to support their development. Thus it seems likely that the composition course—an unnatural but necessary sort of beast—will continue to be the central place where writing instruction occurs. Throughout this book, we will refer often to composition courses and their development. The reader should recall, however, that in our version of a better world, writing would be nurtured throughout the curriculum, without the need for isolated courses.

OTHER PROBLEM AREAS. There are too many additional problem areas and points of disagreement to be detailed here. They range from the theoretical to the practical. Should students be allowed to do "creative" writing in composition courses? What is the relationship of reading to writing? Where does language study fit into a writing program? What can teachers do to help nonwriters? How can you teach writing to nonnative speakers of English? Can you praise students too much?

To some degree, each teacher of writing must ask and answer such questions individually. No final or definitive answer will be found to many of them, either in future research or in classroom experimentation. Further, each teacher must develop a composition philosophy that will allow him or her to work comfortably in the classroom. Such a philosophy ought to be well considered and in keeping with current research. But it will obviously differ from one teacher to another.

Our belief that teaching writing (like learning to write) is idiosyncratic to some degree leads us to suggest a writing assignment for the reader of this book—the only assignment we will make. We suggest that the reader start an informal writing journal, responding and reacting to our statements and assertions, jotting down responses, offering counterarguments, collecting teaching ideas that seem as if they might work well. Kept carefully throughout your reading of the following chapters, this journal can provide a solid foundation for your personal philosophy of writing instruction.

It is an assignment we think you will find not only useful, but authentic.

CHAPTER 2

TEACHING THE COMPOSING PROCESS—FIRST STAGES

Recently we had an opportunity to review a newly published language/composition handbook for secondary school students. Because we were in the midst of preparing materials for this chapter, we naturally looked to see what the book had to say about the writing process. As a matter of fact, it didn't even mention the process, though "Composition" itself occupied one section of the book (one of *eight* sections, a commentary on how much attention textbook writers pay to language study, how little to actual writing). What would a student do, we wondered, if he or she followed the rules, suggestions, and advice offered by this book, touted by the publisher as "the most effective way yet to teach your students the basic skills of reading and writing"?

First, the book suggested, the writer must *choose a purpose*, and in half a paragraph it explained that there are four purposes for writing: to describe, to narrate, to explain, and to persuade. (These four obviously correspond to the traditional four forms of discourse, an obsolete categorization at best.) No further explanation of purpose was given, but the student was asked to demonstrate mastery of the concept by identifying the purpose of a series of sentences.

Next the student was to limit the topic. (Nothing was said of where the topic comes from or how the student could go about finding a good one on his or her own.) An example was given—"Politics"—and the writer was shown how to narrow down this presumably unmanageable topic, first, to "Politics in the USA" (still too broad), eventually to "Politics in My Community" (not at all the same topic the writer began with, in our judgment).

Having a sufficiently narrow topic, the student writer then learned how to prepare a formal outline of the material. The distinction between topic and sentence outlines was given, and the textbook authors recommended the sentence outline because it "supplies more detail." Where, we puzzled, did the detail come from, since the book explained nothing of how to go about finding material and deciding whether or not it fits the composition being planned?

Finally the book moved on to paragraph development, explaining the nature of the topic sentence and showing how it could appear at the beginning, middle, or end of the paragraph.

That pattern of instruction is probably familiar to most readers of this book. It is the traditional approach to composition that has been presented by school textbooks for generations. What is astonishing is that it was presented as a "new" composition program "designed to meet the needs of today's students."

We submit that the textbook does not meet the needs of students today, and, further, that the approach presented there has *never* adequately met the needs of *any* generation of students.

What's so wrong with the traditional approach?

We feel that it fails because it does not talk to students *as writers* and presents almost nothing to guide them through the complex process of composing. The approach was obviously derived by looking at a finished composition—well formed, neatly structured—and then showing students the parts that went into its construction. By analogy, this is a bricklayer approach to architecture that would show the neophyte how a masterpiece like the Taj Mahal was constructed, stone by stone, then tell the apprentice to go out and build something just like it. Returning to writing, the approach advocated by the textbook shows the structures of writing, but not the structuring.

Writing is not like bricklaying or stone masonry, where the final structure is known(or idealized) from the beginning. In creating compositions, writers go through false starts and bad beginnings; they collect quantities of material and use only part of it; they find structures as words flow onto the page. Most important, the final product—the completed essay or poem or story—may provide very few clues about the actual process that went into its creation. It may glitter publicly like the Taj Mahal, but only the writer knows of the sweat that went into it, of the blind passages that were followed, of structures that didn't work out the first, second, or third time.

The alternative to the bricklayer approach that we advocate is described by the title of this chapter:"Teaching the Composing Process." What students need to master is not the blueprints of a few masterworks or set pieces, but skills and processes that will allow them to compose in a variety of situations for a number of purposes.

Teaching this process—or more accurately, the many diverse processes—of composition is difficult. The process differs from one writer to another.

It is evasive, and even established writers have difficulty explaining how they write. In addition, the experienced writer can forget what it is like to be a beginner. Kay Rout (1980) of Michigan State University writes:

> Sometimes the most obvious things, from the point of view of a seasoned veteran, are staggering revelations to the neophyte. When you've been doing something a certain way for so long that you barely notice it any more, like the way you know when a pot of water is hot enough for pasta, it's hard to remember what things seem like to the . . . student writing his first paper. . . (p. 1)

In addition, it may be tempting for the teacher to force students into uniformity. In his otherwise excellent book, *Writing Without Teachers*, Peter Elbow (1973) insists on something called "freewriting." Writers, he says, should let their ideas flow freely, without regard for form or structure. His principle of composition is that once ideas are written down, even in crude form, they can be refined through editing—the "garbage" thrown out. Although we use the freewriting approach ourselves from time to time and recommend it as a prewriting technique, many of our students using Elbow's book complained vociferously that they found the method restricting. Some of those students were uncomfortable because they were "planners," writers who like to work out details in their minds before committing themselves to the page; freewriting made them feel sloppy. Others found that freewriting pushed or rushed them, and they spent so much energy doing freewriting "correctly" that they were not getting down anything of substance. (Still other students, we must add in fairness to Elbow, found freewriting an excellent, liberating strategy.)

There is no single approach to the writing process (or to teaching the writing process) that will work for everyone. Instead of becoming doctrinaire, the teacher might well begin instruction, not by explaining to students how to go through the writing process, but by helping them understand what it is and how they experience it.

UNDERSTANDING THE WRITING PROCESS

Almost every student in any class—elementary school, junior or senior high, college—will have had some previous writing experience, even if poor or unsuccessful. We begin our discussion of the writing process by having the students talk about those experiences and the feelings that went with them. We ask: "How do you feel when a teacher says, 'I want you to write . . .'?" This question allows students to describe some of their apprehensions about writing, and almost every student in the class will describe feelings of fear and inadequacy, sometimes even of dread.

"Do you postpone writing assignments?" is another question that can elicit a useful response. We freely admit to our students that we procrastinate over writing tasks, finding all kinds of excuses, including taking down or putting up those wretched storm windows, as ways of avoiding that initial confrontation with the blank page. "Why do we all seem to feel that way?" we ask. "We don't block when it comes time to talk. Why is it so much different when we have to put words down on paper?"

Then the responses come. "I can't spell and don't know how to look things up." "My teacher last year told me that my writing wasn't so hot." "I don't know, except that I really dread it—I'll do anything rather than write."

We encourage students by explaining that most writers, even solid professionals, have those feelings. In many classes we've read a passage from Steinbeck's *Sweet Thursday* in which Doc postpones and fidgets over a writing assignment, eventually distracting himself by thinking about a pretty girl's legs. (See Watkins and Knight, 1966.)

Not all writers (and students) have negative feelings about the writing process, and in empathizing with fears and apprehensions, it is important not to overemphasize them. We encourage students to talk positively about their writing experiences as well. "What's the best paper you've ever written? Why was it successful for you?" "Does anybody in here like to write stories or poems? How did you get started?" "Has anyone written for a newspaper—perhaps a hand-published newsletter when you were younger or a high school or college paper? What did you find satisfying about that?"

Eventually we move beyond this discussion of feelings to talk about writing habits. This discussion can range from the nuts-and-bolts of materials ("Do you write in pencil or pen or [for older students] in typewriter?" "Do you write on legal pads or notebook sheets or old envelopes?") to the conditions under which people like to write ("Where do you write? When do you write? Do you have a special place where you like to go? Do you work best at morning or night? Can you work with the radio or TV on? Do you have to have silence to write?"). It is important for students to realize that every person develops a unique pattern for going about writing, and knowing that, students can seek out their own best circumstances and conditions. Further, this information can be very useful to the instructor in determining how to create a classroom environment that fosters or promotes writing.

Next on our agenda comes talk of the writing process itself: finding ideas, gathering materials, forming plans, writing, revising, polishing. Not all students know that writing is generally completed in stages. Too often their previous writing assignments have been one-shot affairs—writing answers to examination questions, for example, or doing study questions. In reviewing the results of the National Assessment of Writing, a writing sample designed to reveal the abilities of 9-, 12-, and 17-year-olds and young adults aged 26 to 35, John C. Maxwell (1973) commented that NAEP revealed:

that multitudes of Americans are not aware that revision is a major part of the process called writing.

He remarked that although students taking some versions of the NAEP were given specific instructions to revise their papers, most either did not revise or limited their changes to corrections of spelling and punctuation.

To show students that there is more to writing than simply completing a single draft—first, last, and only—we bring in materials we have generated in preparing papers, everything from notes and marked up, cut-and-pasted drafts to the final copy, whether typewritten or published. We talk about how that piece of writing came into being—where the idea came from, how it grew, how it changed and was shaped through various stages of the writing process.

There is a danger here: One can make the writing process appear overwhelmingly complex and thus intimidate students—"I could never do anything like that." At the same time, we think it is useful for students to see that their teachers write, too. As a way of setting their minds at rest, we explain that we don't expect seventh graders or tenth graders or college freshmen to put in as much time as we do in our own professional writing. "But," we add, "the basic stages that we go through—planning, drafting, revising—are the same ones you use when writing."

Perhaps even better than using either one's own writing is to get students themselves to save notes and drafts to show other students. Such materials can be used to create an interesting bulletin board display. Tape recorded commentary by the student writers describing how they wrote can be a valuable supplement to the documentary evidence provided by drafts and notes.

It is also useful with some classes, particularly upper-level high school and college, to have the students collect and evaluate the advice they have been given about writing. We are continually astonished by the nuggets of wisdom (more often, ignorance) that students bring to our writing classes. "Never begin a sentence with 'but'," is advice that is commonly given, though our regular arbiter of usage, Rudolf Flesch, says in his *Look it Up: A Deskbook of American Spelling and Style* (1977), "The idea that *but* should not be used is pure superstition. Follow the example of the Bible, which says 'But Jesus gave him no answer' (John 19:9)." The students learn "Never use first person pronouns in an essay" by teachers who forget that the noun, *essay*, began as a Latin verb, *esso*, "I try." "Always outline before you write" is taught in classrooms across the country, but almost every group of students we have taught includes a number of people who, when asked to turn in outlines, would write the essay first and then outline it afterward.

The point of this activity is not to belittle previous teachers or to make a mockery of them. Instead, it is to give the students a little reality therapy about the composing process. It is difficult to teach writing to students who have mistaken notions about "good" writing or about how to tackle the writing process. Thus we encourage them to sort the good advice they have received from the bad, testing it against their own experience as writers.

To continue that focus throughout the course, we often have students keep a writer's log or writer's notebook. The contents of these journals can vary widely. Students can jot down notes and observations for their papers. They can use the log as a place to write rough drafts. One section, however, ought to be reserved for the students' comments about the writing process itself. After completing an assignment, for instance, the students might write a page describing the "pleasures and pains" of the activity, describing what went well or smoothly and what did not. They can make notes on strategies that worked for them in particular papers, and they can record techniques that helped them write better—even changing from a ball-point to a felt tip pen. From time to time during the writing course, the teacher can ask students to discuss their jottings in this section of the writer's log so that the class, not just the individual, can benefit from a growing body of knowledge—gained through actual experience—about the process of composition.

THE ENVIRONMENT FOR COMPOSING

Helping students learn about the nature of the composing process is a part of setting the stage—preparing students for actual writing that is to follow. The classroom environment is also a part of stage setting, creating the mood and tone of the place where the drama of writing will happen. Too often the setting is ignored by teachers.

To write successfully, one must feel reasonably comfortable with one's environment, both physical and spiritual. Professional writers work hard to find a place where they can habitually write with a degree of comfort and security. (Tidbit: "Norman Mailer's writing carrel is accessible only by walking across a six-inch wide plank with a ten-foot drop below. This hazardous arrangement, he once explained, prevents him from trying to write at times when he's too drunk to walk a straight line." [Felton and Fowler, 1980.]) Whether students are doing most of their writing inside the classroom or elsewhere, the class—more than a room, a gathering of people in a room—plays a powerful role in determining how well or badly the students write. Indeed, if the classroom environment is conducive to writing, students will learn much more about the actual process of composition than they might in a place where they feel uncomfortable or where writing seems unnatural.

The following suggestions can help the writing teacher set the stage, whether it be a self-contained elementary school classroom with carpeted floor and movable furniture or a stern and barren classroom in the oldest building on a college campus.

1. *Make the class a place where writing is expected as a part of the natural order of things.* A colleague at Michigan State University, Chris Clark (1980) of the Institute for Research on Teaching, has found that children write more freely than usual when they learn from the very first day that writing is a natural, useful mode of communication, and that, to participate fully in the class, they must write regularly. Too often writing is isolated in special days (Friday is theme day) or used only peripherally in instruction (Writing is something you do only on tests). Clark suggests that elementary children should write constantly—notes, journals, diaries, stories, reports—and that the teacher should make a point of showing them how writing functions as a major form of communication in the school.

At the college level, Peter Elbow (1979) notes that often teachers require writing only for the sake of requiring writing—that is, to teach composition. The students do not learn that writing is good for something: generating ideas, accomplishing tasks, communicating with people. He suggests, for example, that teachers have their students:

Write responses to classroom lectures or discussions.

Write as a warm-up prior to class discussions.

Write to "real world" audiences: employers, school administrators, newspaper editors, politicians, business people.

Write about what they are learning in a course.

Share knowledge with one another through writing.

In Chapters 6 and 7 we will show in more detail how writing activities can be woven into a variety of courses and programs, both in English and in other subject areas. For the moment, it is enough to stress that as soon as students enter a classroom they should learn: "In this class, we write."

Not all students will welcome this opportunity to write. Frederick Ross, a college biology teacher who enjoys teaching writing, reports that when he describes the amount of writing to be done in his course, some students drop it and move to other sections where short-answer and multiple-guess questions are the rule (Ross and Jarosz, 1978). Of course, in the schools students seldom have the luxury of changing sections, but they convey their unhappiness about having to write in other ways. Still, as Ross reports, the students who stay with him come to recognize the value of what he is doing. When writing is taught well and made a satisfying experience for students, they learn to value it more highly. When they do, they have taken a major step toward being practicing writers, not just students of writing.

2. *Make the class a place where writing need not be feared.* The apprehension of Fred Ross's students and millions of others is understandable. In the past, writing has often been a threat, even a punishment. There has been little joy associated with writing assignments, and the penalties for failing to write well range from bad grades to public humiliation.

Larry Levinger (1978), a professional writer as well as a teacher of writing, remarks:

> *It may be safe to say that the poor writing student has, at some critical stage in his life, experienced trauma in his attempts to communicate, and has, as a result, turned off to the natural and authentic elements of language.* (p. 28)

"Trauma" may seem too strong a word. But it is an accurate description of many students' past experiences, and, for many others, words such as "unsettling," "discouraging," "frightening," and "embarrassing" may seem appropriate.

We don't want to overemphasize the negative sides to writing. We don't want to give the impression that *all* students have been traumatized by bad writing experiences; nor do we wish to overstress the "agonies" of the composing process.

At the same time, any teacher interested in helping students learn to write better will have to face up to the fact that a range of negative feelings may exist in the class.

Making the writing class "safe" is no easy task. On the opening day of our classes (and on many days thereafter) we find ways of telling students, first, that we do not regard writing as a life-and-death affair, and, second, that we are basically much more interested in their growth as individuals than in their met or unmet potential as writers.

We say that we consider the writing class to be a kind of laboratory (or greenhouse, to pick up a metaphor we used in Chapter 1), a place where people can experiment and grow. We urge students to try new things with writing—to tackle new discourse forms, to try to reach audiences they have never written for before. We also stress that we are much more interested in finding and supporting successes than in pointing out weaknesses and failures. Growth in writing, we explain, seems to come about best when writers learn to do things right, not when they have done them wrong.

The first set of papers is a test for both the students and the instructor. The students know that one way or another they are being sized up. (Many of them have written on "My Summer Vacation" several times, and they know precisely why that theme is assigned on the first day of school: to find out how well or badly they write.) The teacher will be tested, too, for the students will study his or her comments when the themes are returned and consciously or unconsciously size up the teacher and determine if he or she is "safe" to be with.

Human relations handbooks are filled with advice and suggestions on how to build trust between student and teacher. In the writing class, the most important ingredient, it seems to us, is whether the teacher takes a positive attitude toward the students. We believe that students of all ages are basically capable creatures who are interested in learning and in bettering themselves. We find that if we can communicate that belief to the students, they tend to trust us, and at that point, the writing class becomes safe.

Or, perhaps better, the writing class becomes safer.

For the teacher is not the only person in the class who must be trusted. The students must learn to trust and to work with one another, and in the highly competitive school environment, trust and cooperation are not come by easily.

To build trust, we use a great deal of collaborative and small group work in our writing courses. Students talk with one another while planning papers; they discuss notes and outlines; they share first, second, and third drafts; they edit and critique one another's papers. It takes time to build these group skills, because often students have spent much of their time in teacher-dominated classrooms where cooperation with fellow students has been irrelevant. But students' confidence in one another comes—with time, with patience, and, above all, with the commitment of the teacher to its importance.

3. *Make the classroom a place where the raw materials of writing are readily available.* Our ideal writing classroom exists in a nearby elementary school. It is a well lighted, fully carpeted room with furniture that can be moved about. In addition to conventional school desks—clustered in fours to create work tables and conversation centers—the room is furnished with an old sofa, two armchairs, and several vinyl beanbag chairs—probably garage sale remnants—and these have been placed in corners to create comfortable places for students to write. A supply of lap boards cut from sheets of masonite is also available for armchair writers. Three walls are covered with cork boards, and the teacher keeps students' written work in constant, but changing display. In a small cabinet she has placed writing supplies: a box of pens and pencils, colored and plain; stacks of paper, colored and plain; an old but functional Royal typewriter that can be pulled out and placed on a student's desk; art supplies for decorating and binding final copies. Book-shelves and spinner racks contain books and magazines, a classroom library of perhaps two hundred titles, including books that the students themselves have written. Along the back wall is a reference shelf, with almanacs, ency-clopedias, the *Guiness Book of World Records* (the most frequently thumbed book in the place), and dictionaries.

Students find it a pleasant place in which to write.

People who hear about that room remark that it sounds like many elementary school classrooms they have seen, but that it is unlike many junior high, most senior high, and virtually all college classrooms. Of course, teaching conditions at those upper levels are different. Not all high school teachers have a permanently assigned room in which to teach. Virtually all college professors must move from one classroom to another and must concentrate on excusing their Comp 101 students by 9:55 sharp so the Econ 206 people can use the space at 10. Under such circumstances, creating a room environment conducive to writing is extremely difficult. At the same time, we think the elementary teacher's room should be kept in mind as a model, and teachers should try to approximate it, adapting whatever physical facilities they find themselves in to make a comfortable, inviting environment for writing.

4. *Provide teacher support for writers.* "Environment" is obviously more than just classroom space and furniture. Good writing classes can be taught even in the bleakest of physical settings, provided the intellectual and spiritual environment is right. No factor is more important than the attitude the teacher takes toward students. We have suggested that it is important for the writing teacher to believe that students are capable of writing well. The other side of that coin is that teachers must be willing to do the work, to provide the support, to help, cajole, and encourage students into writing as well as they can.

It seems to be an occupational hazard among writing teachers that they talk about how poorly their students write. In faculty lounges one regularly hears war stories—horror stories—about the odd, strange, and incoherent things students write. Faculty newsletters regularly contain examples of student illiteracies, displayed for the amusement of other teachers, who are aghast.

It is understandable that composition teachers grow weary of seeing the same or similar errors repeated time and again by students. We know the frustration of reading multiple batches of themes that lack coherence, grace, style, and substance.

At the same time, it seems to us that the public undercutting of students' writing is symptomatic of a deeper problem: an unwillingness of teachers to *teach*, to provide the help and support that students need to learn to write better. We also believe that a teacher's willingness (or unwillingness) to teach is communicated very quickly to students and that it strongly affects their performance. Young people will write and write well in the classes of teachers whom they see as helpful and supportive. If the teacher is a doubter of their abilities and conveys a "show me" or "you'll have to get this on your own" attitude, they tend to write poorly.

We do not mean to imply that the teacher must go to extraordinary lengths to cater to individual student problems. The teacher should not feel compelled to take late night phone calls the day before a paper is due or to spend long hours outside the class tutoring. But it seems to us important that the writing teacher recognize that the students who come to class will, for the most part, *not* be good writers. They will be underprepared and inexperienced. Even those who have a reasonable degree of fluency may have problems with content, style, and audience. All of them need the kind of individualized help and support a good writing teacher can give them.

5. *Create the structure and tone of a writing workshop.* Many of the writing assignments a person receives in his or her lifetime call for impromptu composition:

"I'll need your report on this by 2 o'clock sharp."

"Send a memo out on this will you? Right away!"

"Describe the principal causes of the fall of the Roman Empire (30 minutes)."

Thus the writing of impromptu themes is occasionally valuable, good practice for real world writing experiences.

At the same time, impromptu writing assignments—calling for writing to be done on the spur of the moment with little time for planning or revision—often invite *bad* writing. Professional writers regularly comment on how slowly writing comes, on how often they have to revise to create a satisfactory piece. It seems unfortunate that the schools, in general, and writing classes, in particular, place so much emphasis on instant writing. (See Judy, "On Clock Watching and Composing," 1968)

Taking a workshop—or "wordshop"—approach to writing simply means providing adequate time for students to experience all aspects of the writing process: time to find and generate ideas, time to size up and assess an audience, time to plan, time to write and revise, time to respond to one another's work and to prepare it for a wider readership. Of course, not all of these stages must take place inside the classroom. Planning will often take students to the library for work; writing may be better done at home or in the dormitory than in the class; revision may need to be done in private rather than in small groups. But the writing class remains the center, the focal point of activity. It is the place where the assignment begins and ends, and it is the place where much of the crafting of writing is done.

Further, the workshop approach provides teachers with time to give the support and help referred to in the previous section. By taking time to work with students at all phases of the writing process, teachers can provide assistance to individual students: the help Bill needs in sharpening an idea, the discussion Regina needs to work out her basic plan, the proofreading help Jack requires to get his paper publication-ready.

The workshop approach also makes it easier for teachers to differentiate assignments and to offer a variety of writing options. There seems to be no real reason why all students must write on the same topic at the same time. In the workshop, students can tackle a range of topics and complete their work in phases and at various times (something that can also ease the paper grading burden for the teacher). Some teachers we know have students maintain a "works in progress" file, where they keep several pieces in various stages of completion.

Establishing a writing workshop obviously requires a greater commitment of time to writing than is ordinarily given in the schools, but, as our bias toward learning through experience should make clear, we think that time is well spent. In taking ample time for a writing activity—perhaps days or even weeks—the teacher helps to insure that the final product, the students' writing, will be as good as they can make it.

Often, something has to "give" in the curriculum for workshop time to be found. Our candidate for getting the ax is the peripheral drill that is so often a part of writing courses: spelling lessons, vocabulary lessons, grammar exercises, sentence combining activities. As is probably clear, the workshop approach allows most of these matters to be taken up in process, as the need for instruction occurs, so that nothing is truly lost when the workshop is introduced.

6. *Make the composition class a forum for the exchange and development of ideas.* The essential philosophical tenet underlying this book is that *ideas* and *experience* are the driving force behind good writing. When a person wants to develop and share an idea with another person, he or she begins shaping and structuring papers and thus learns something of structure and organization. When a person has an experience to describe, he or she begins searching for right words, good words to tell about it and thus begins to shape a writing style. In our naturalistic approach, substance and content are absolutely essential. As Wendell Johnson has suggested, one can't "write writing"; one writes ideas, experiences, and thoughts.

Thus the writing class should be more than just a wordshop, more than just a place for the writing of papers. It should be an intellectually rich center of discussion and debate. The teacher of a course called "composition" must be careful not to let the concern for developing writing skills become removed from the ideas and experiences that make up and lead to good writing. If the students' experiences are attended to, much else in the writing course follows naturally.

CLASSROOM TECHNIQUES FOR TEACHING THE WRITING PROCESS

GENERATION AND FOCUS. Those two words are used by Richard Gebhardt (1977), Director of the Writing Program of Findlay College, to replace the conventional term "organization." He suggests that even after students have found the basic idea for a paper they need help that is more than just information about organizational patterns or structures. Writers must *generate* additional material, for their ideas are seldom sufficiently formed or detailed to create a good paper instantly. Further, writers must *focus* their ideas, selecting from all the material they have available and deciding how to present it in a coherent fashion.

We like to use a series of questions that a rhetorician would call a *heuristic* or *discovery procedure* that helps students synthesize what they know and don't know about their subject and then plan their paper to meet the needs of their audience:

1. *What do you already know about the subject?* Remember that even on topics involving original research, students already have some background information. (If they have none, the topic may be too advanced for them.) Here the students simply jot down a few sentences summarizing their existing knowledge.)

2. *What would you like to find out about the topic?* Or, *what don't you know?* The student lists questions, as many as possible, describing what he or she would like to learn or find out. These questions can be clustered along similar lines or boiled down into three or four major or key questions.

3. *Where can you find out answers?* Books are an obvious answer in English classes, but too often teachers neglect more convenient resources: other people. At this point in the heuristic, the students brainstorm for possible information sources—books, magazines, films, television, recordings, experts, friends, teachers, parents. By the time this list is completed, it ought to be evident to the students where to turn next. (Note: Not all writing topics will involve this informal "research" phase. In the case of personal experience papers, no research at all may be necessary.)

4. *Given what you know, what would you like to share with your readers?* This question is raised only after the students have generated all the material they need. It causes them to focus and to begin paring down their material by asking them to consider the needs and interests of their audience.

5. *Put yourself in the place of your reader. In what order would you want to learn about your information?* (Alternatively: *With your reader in mind, what would be the most interesting or logical order in which to present your*

ideas?) The students move toward sequencing and structuring their papers.

This heuristic is not foolproof, and students can come up blank in response to some of the questions. In addition, this procedure is best suited to expository writing, and teachers need to adapt it for use with other writing forms and genres. But we find that it is successful in getting students to generate and organize material by encouraging them to draw, first, on their own knowledge, and, second, on what they perceive to be the needs of their readers. It will not produce anything so rigid as a formal outline, but it will lead students to a detailed set of notes and a plan of attack for the paper.

As a footnote we should add that we do not think students should be required to have a fixed or rigid plan in mind before writing. Writing itself is a process of learning and discovery. Once the general plan has been formed, we suggest that students get on with the writing itself. At that time the "bugs" in their plan, the holes in their knowledge, the additional needs of readers, will become more obvious.

INITIATING AND SUSTAINING THE FLOW OF WRITING.   When the planning is done, it's time to write. The student has picked a topic and done some work generating and focusing ideas. There is a plan of attack in mind. The writer picks up pen and paper and . . . finds something else to do— *anything* else. Writer's block, or, more simply, trouble in getting started is common enough among both professional and novice writers, and whole books have been written about it. (See, for instance, Mack and Skjei, *Overcoming Writing Blocks*, 1979.) The problems of the professional writer have been thoroughly described in a number of places; research on young writers' blocks is not prolific.

It is evident that many problems for the novice may grow from the nature of the writing assignment itself, an assignment that may be inappropriate, beyond the student's knowledge or experience, devoted to testing and examining rather than learning, or without obvious purpose or audience. Past bad experiences with writing may intervene, so that the students are reluctant to expose themselves on paper. Overinstruction in basics is often a cause of student writing blocks, with fear of making spelling and usage mistakes taking precedence in the writer's mind over communicating with an audience.

But assuming that none of these is a factor, students still have many problems initiating a flow of writing and then sustaining it, and there are a number of techniques teachers can suggest that will enable students to move past the blinding whiteness of the page and to get the pen moving.

For instance, earlier we were critical of Peter Elbow's insistence on freewriting as a fixed component of the writing process. However, some (but not necessarily all) writers find *freewriting* a good way to begin. "Write down anything," the teacher can say. "Let the pen flow. Paper is cheap and you can always discard the writing that is bad." In fact, Elbow suggests that revision is, in effect, nothing more than separating the garbage from the good stuff produced through freewriting.

Other teachers talk of *nonstop writing* or *free association*. The student writes a topic or title at the top of the page and simply writes down whatever comes to mind. Some teachers suggest that if the student gets stuck, he or she should just keep writing the last word over and over until something comes to mind.

Freewriting and free association do not usually produce solid, well-organized first drafts. They help the writer get material down on paper, but it may not be good or readable material. (Herum and Cummings (1971) recommend telling students that they can write a "zero draft," something that is prior to a "first draft.") We prefer to treat freewriting not as a draft, but as part of the process of generating ideas. But again, we must emphasize that freewriting or nonstop writing works to break blocks for some writers. It is worth describing for students.

At the opposite end of the spectrum from the freewriters are the "incredibly careful" writers. These are people who are uncomfortable putting down "garbage" and want to write something that is fairly close to final copy. They may well block on writing the first paragraph, unable to think about the composition as a whole until they have gotten paragraph one down. For them, *oral composition* may be helpful, with the teacher having them talk through the beginning, line by line, with another person so that the details are worked out before words are actually committed to paper. Art Spikol (1980) of the Philadelphia Writers School suggests that professionals draft five or more openings for an article before selecting one as the definitive paragraph. Such a technique might work for the incredibly careful writer as well.

Other people can unblock by ignoring the opening paragraph altogether. We regularly suggest that our students start writing in the middle. "If you can't get started at the beginning, start anyplace else. Find a paragraph or an idea that you're ready to get down and write it. You can fill in the rest later." This technique works, it seems to us, because often a writer doesn't know what the opening or lead should be until the entire piece is finished.

In our own writing, we frequently use the first paragraph as a kind of "throwaway." We begin writing with the full intention of making the beginning a good one, yet because of first draft jitters, that paragraph often wanders. In revising, we frequently discard the opening lines, finding that the piece doesn't get down to business until later.

An unblocking technique that is widely used in the elementary schools and deserves application at upper levels is *dictation*. For many writers, handwriting and transcription skills may be a major block in writing. That is, the student has plenty to say but has difficulty with the mechanical act of getting it down on paper. While obviously every writer needs to master transcription skills at some point, the philosophy behind this technique argues that lack of these skills should never be allowed to interfere with the more basic skill of communicating ideas. If students learn that they can shape their ideas orally, they can gradually build the handwriting and spelling skills that will let them make the transition to writing.

Obviously, taking dictation is time consuming, usually requiring a teacher, teacher aide, or an older student to work one-to-one with the writer. Too, some students at the upper levels of the school system might be embarrassed by dictation, finding it babyish. A solution to both problems may be found in the *tape recorder:* The students record what they have to say, then replay it, in essence taking their own dictation. There is also a danger in that technique because the recording itself may be rambling and diffuse—characteristic of oral language—so that the written version might not be particularly good. Still, in the spirit of this chapter, we suggest that teachers discuss the technique with students. In most any class, it will work for one or several students.

The basic techniques we have described seem to serve successfully, alone or in combination, for helping most writers initiate the flow. If a teacher encounters insoluble problems, he or she might want to study a specialized book on writer's block like Mack and Skjei's.

Sustaining the flow is generally easier than initiating it. We find that it is relatively rare for students to reach a dead end in the middle of a composition, though they may encounter temporary roadblocks or quite simply run out of gas as they come near the end of the road.

Establishing the class as a writing workshop seems to us vital at this point. Although the students may do some writing outside of class, they should also bring their work to class to discuss it while it is still in the process of being shaped and formed. Generally, a writing workshop will be individualized, recognizing that various writers go through the process in different ways. The teacher plays the role of a manager/consultant, helping students organize their approach to the writing process and consulting with them about the words they have put and are putting on paper.

Typically, a writing workshop might have students engaged in:

Writing a zero or first draft.

Talking with one another about plans, drafts, or revision.

Conferring with the teacher about individual problems.

Sharing completed work in small groups.

Polishing papers to make them ready for public reading or publication.

The writing workshop is not a quiet place where one hears only the scratching of pens on paper or wet thumbs flicking through dictionary pages. It should be considerately abubble with conversation about all phases of the writing process. It is the time and place when and where students learn most about the process of composing.

RESPONSE AND FEEDBACK. Chapter 5 will examine this topic in detail, and we will just touch on it briefly here. Making the writing process authentic for students means that the response and reaction they receive to their papers must be authentic as well. It is not encouraging to a young writer to slave away at preparing a composition only to discover that the only reader is the teacher, whose only interest is in mechanical correctness and rhetorical accuracy. For us the writing workshop/wordshop creates a natural way of bringing authenticity into the writing process, for as students write and revise, they discuss their papers freely and openly. As we will show, with just a little training students can comfortably serve as audiences for one another's completed pieces, partially relieving the teacher of the burden of theme correcting. But audiences for student writing ought to extend beyond the classroom as well, a topic we will explore in greater depth in Chapter 6.

CHAPTER 3

WRITING ASSIGNMENTS AND ACTIVITIES

As we observed in Chapter 1, for over one hundred years in the teaching of writing instruction focused on four "forms of discourse," usually described as *narration, description, argumentation,* and *exposition.* The students were given an explanation or analysis of each mode and occasionally shown examples demonstrating the characteristics of the mode. After students heard or read about the explication they were asked to produce their own essay of narration, description, argumentation, or exposition.

There are several flaws in this approach to assigning writing to students, but we would like to focus on just two. First, the modal approach falsifies and distorts both the purpose and the function of most writers' works. James Britton (1975), the British researcher and theorist, describes how complex the labeling of modes of discourse really is:

> It is no difficult matter to find narrative or descriptive writing which has as its dominant function calculated persuasion or highly didactic explanation. Only by giving narrative and description sharply different functions could the system be made consistent and workable. . . . Writing characterized as "narration" and writing characterized as "description" may well be performing the same function for the writer; on the other hand, two pieces put into the same category might well differ widely in the kinds of demands they make on the writer: the broad category "exposition" for example would embrace tasks as far apart as simple technical explanation and the elaboration of a complex theory. (p. 5)

The common technique of isolating passages of writing to demonstrate a particular mode misleads students about the nature of writing and the writing process, particularly in today's world where narrative and descriptive elements are becoming more widely used in so-called expository and argumentative writings in popular and professional publications.

A second, more significant, problem with the modal approach is that it falsifies the way in which writers write. The real writer doesn't begin by deciding that a piece of narration or description or exposition is what he or she wants to do. The writer begins with an idea, an insight, a perception, an observation, something to share with an audience. After talking, thinking, and planning, the writer writes. And as all of these things—from experiencing to writing—take place, a point of view, a pattern, and sequence emerge. The writing takes on form.

Gregory and Elizabeth Cowan (1980) describe the process this way:

> Nobody is sure exactly how writers decide the form that their writing will finally take. Usually a writer doesn't really decide. The essay, once the thesis is thought out, seems to take its form organically. This means that the purpose the writer has for doing the writing and the thesis (or the point of the writing) somehow determine the form of the essay. Form is often a subconscious or automatic activity with experienced writers. (p. 139)

Many programs purporting to teach writing are starting in the wrong place with their emphasis on mode. We believe, conversely, that the good writing assignment places the emphasis on the student as a thinker and on the development of his or her thoughts from the inception of the idea to the communication to an audience. According to Eleanor Hoffman and John Schifsky, who are teachers of composition at the University of Minnesota (Duluth) and Scholastica College of Duluth, respectively (1977):

> A good writing assignment recognizes all the student's needs and his developmental maturity. It provides needed guidance from the prewriting through the writing stages. It provides a definite route through the assignment, a route which enables the student to arrive at his destination. A productive and useful assignment requires planning that structures the assignment for both teacher and student. (p. 41)

What they are describing is obviously much more complex than the conventional school theme assignment. Hoffman and Schifsky recognize that for a writing assignment to be successful, it must provide guidance for students at all phases of the writing process, from collecting ideas to receiving the response of a readership.

We prefer the term "writing activity" to "writing assignment," and our choice is not simply a matter of euphemism. "Assignment" sounds more demanding than "activity," but, more important, "assignment" seems to imply that the teacher's job is complete once the writing task has been described to the students. Further, "assignment" sounds limited and one dimensional, where a writing activity—a good one, at least—ought to provide possibilities that lead the students off in many directions.

But whether one chooses to call them assignments or activities, the heart of teaching the composing process is what the students actually do with language in response to the suggestions, commands, or invitations of the teacher. It is when students *write* that their skills grow and develop. Thus the design of the writing activity is crucial. If the activity is a good one, it will initiate a flow of writing and provide students the help they need to complete it successfully. If it fails to initiate the flow, or if the teacher fails to supply the necessary support, the activity will fail and little or no learning will take place.

In an attempt to describe and define the dimensions of good or successful writing assignments or activities, Gilbert Tierney of Harper College, Palatine, Illinois, and Stephen Judy (1972) asked a number of secondary school and college teachers to rate hypothetical assignments and to describe the criteria used in making the judgment. They found that the criteria experienced teachers use fell into two major categories. The first of these focused on the relationship between the writer and the assignment or the material. In broadest terms, the criteria ask, "How does the activity engage the student writer in the process of composing?":

Motivation and Stimulation. *Does the assignment provide enough direction that students can write without feeling hopelessly lost? Does it avoid channelling all students into making a single kind of composition, response, or statement? Is this activity one for which the students have enough knowledge to write freely (e.g., a personal experience) or one for which they can find ideas and materials readily? Is it basically interesting and potentially rewarding, enough so that kids will choose to do it rather than simply seeing it as one more routine classroom exercise?*

Appropriateness. *Are the subject and form appropriate to the age, maturity, and background of the students? Does the assignment allow the student to "be himself," without forcing him into a premature, false adulthood?*

Open-endedness. *Is the assignment structured to provide for a divergence of forms and responses (e.g., an essay, play, poem, or nonverbal composition)? Does it include options for students with varying interests and levels of verbal skill, providing opportunities for the more able to stretch their energies and skills while providing opportunities for the less able to succeed?*

Language Play. *Is the assignment designed to encourage the students to try something new—a technique, a tone of voice, a genre (e.g., dialogue, satire, poem)? Can they feel free to "fool around" a bit, searching for new and interesting ideas, voices, and styles without fear of being penalized?* (p. 267)

The other criteria teachers described centered on the relationship between the student writer and his or her audience. In essence, they asked, "Does the activity provide an opportunity for the student to write for a genuine audience?":

> The Writer's Function. *Is the student helped to see the kinds of roles and possible approaches that are open to him as a writer? Can he find out what he needs to know and do to succeed? Does the assignment or classroom setting provide ways in which the student can explore or discover approaches without spending undue time simply guessing what might be appropriate?*
>
> Voice. *Is the student asked to write in a voice that is natural to him? Is he asked to sound like someone he is not (e.g., a college professor)? Is he allowed to make his attitude toward his audience and subject clear?*
>
> Readers. *Is a real audience, one important to the writer, provided for the paper? Is the writer aware of who his audience will be?*
>
> Reactions. *Are provisions made for the members of the audience to talk to the writer about the paper and their reading of it? Can the writer get real reactions rather than academic criticism alone? Can he develop a sense of pleasure and satisfaction over sharing his work with others?* (pp. 268–269)

Obviously, meeting all those criteria in a single writing activity is a tall order, and few assignments will satisfy all of them. In fact, even an activity that seems to meet all the criteria successfully may, in actual practice, fall short and lead to an unproductive classroom experience. Teachers must experiment, thoughtfully and carefully, to come up with assignments and activities that work for them.

At this point we would like to outline five categories of writing activities that seem to us successful in not only getting students to write, but helping them to write better. The activities extend across a range of writing, beginning with personal, sometimes private writing and moving toward public forms. The sequence of the categories can also serve as a pattern for organizing a writing course, a topic we will discuss in more detail in Chapter 7 and illustrate in Appendix A with one of our own course syllabi. The categories are:

1. Opening up
2. Exploring the self
3. Writing about oneself and others
4. Exploring problems, issues, and values
5. Investigating/probing/researching

OPENING UP

Often we have heard instructors complaining about their students, "They don't have any ideas. I'll teach them form and structure and then when they have some ideas, they'll be able to put them into some sort of readable form." In addition to demonstrating ignorance about how ideas are born and develop, such statements demonstrate a lack of regard for and understanding of the developing writer. The difficulty students have in knowing what to write about—a fairly common problem—often stems from the fact that students have been told what to write—usually canned assignments from textbooks—throughout much of their schooling. Students have not been asked to think about what they have to say and to whom they have to say it. Even when an assignment given by the teacher is one that the students enjoy and can complete successfully, part of the value of writing is lost if the students do not make basic choices about the topic and do not write about material that is vital to them as individuals.

Among the important things that writing teaches—or writing teachers can teach—is for students to rely on their ability to discover what they believe and know. When done for reasons important to the writer, not just to please the teacher, writing can help the writer develop a sense of self, some convictions, and a depth of thought and feeling. It seems important, then, for the teacher to help young writers work on the stuff of their own experience.

Students sometimes resist opening up about personal concerns and experiences for fear of being ridiculed, rejected, or red pencilled. Often, too, students haven't consciously analyzed their experiences, values, or ideas so that they feel they have enough control over them to write. Sometimes they do not consider their experiences unique or interesting; sometimes they do not feel that their beliefs are appropriate for school or college writing. Part of the teacher's task in designing writing activities is to help students discover what they can write about, what they want to write about.

In the early phases of most courses, students have a tendency to be cautious with language. While their language outside the classroom is natural and even playful, their choice of language in school is tense and constrained. Teachers can use writing activities to help students play with language, manipulating words and meanings, creating different voices and styles. They should learn early in the course that their natural voice is appropriate for most writing assignments, and they should discover that they can exploit language rather than feel that it controls them.

Early writing activities can also help students open up to one another. At the beginning of the writing class, students often feel hesitant about exposing their ideas to others. Teachers ought to create activities to ease the students into sharing their ideas and their writings with one another.

Interest inventories provide one way of helping students develop lists of possible writing topics. The following is one we have used with both secondary and college students:

EPISODES AND INTERESTS: Some Starting Points for Writing

Your own experiences, ideas, adventures, interests, and misadventures are the starting point for good writing. Here are a few categories where you probably have ideas and stories well worth writing about. Under each category, jot down the significant incidents and episodes in your life.

EARLY CHILDHOOD. Things you did when you were younger and wiser (or not as wise as you thought). Memories of family. Things you did that scared the daylights out of grown-ups. Holidays. Disappointments. Being ill. Being happy.

PEOPLE. Friends, enemies, rivals, unforgettable characters, relatives, people who frightened you, people who supported you.

FOND MEMORIES. Moments you'd like to relive.

NOT-SO-FOND MEMORIES. Never again.

ARGUMENTS, QUARRELS, AND FIGHTS.

FIRSTS. First love, first movie, first experience with death, first snowfall, first day at school.

SCHOOL. Academic and nonacademic concerns. The library. Favorite classes. Sports. The trouble with this place is: _____.

OUTSIDE INTERESTS. Special areas of interest and skills beyond the halls of school.

OPTIONS. What are the possibilities you see for yourself in coming years? School. Jobs. Family.

CONTEMPORARY CULTURE. What are your interests in books? in films? in music?

LANDMARKS. Each of us has a number of landmarks or turning points in his or her life. Moments of truth. Crucial decisions. Meeting the right or wrong person. Make a list of the landmarks in your life. (The list might even look like the table of contents for your autobiography.)

After you have finished jotting down ideas in each category, run through the list a second time. Place a check or an asterisk by each topic that especially interests you or that you think might interest your classmates. Those will be especially good topics for writing.

We find such inventories can easily provide a storehouse of writing topics for the first half of a course. Once we have had students complete the inventory, we also spend time in class encouraging small group discussions about it. "Share some of your outside interests. Describe to each other your childhood antics and pranks." The discussion helps the students see that they do, in fact, have many things within their experience that can be shared with an audience.

Another starting point for writing is to have students investigate identity and self-awareness. In *Composition for Personal Growth*, Robert Hawley, Sidney Simon, and D.D. Britton (1973) suggest four categories: *patterns and preferences, influences, competencies,* and *body.* Students make lists of their own interests, values, or experiences for each. Under *influences,* for example, students are asked to list the names of ten peers and ten adults for whom they have great respect and to describe the qualities they value in each. Students then compare the two lists and explain what they discovered about themselves. The authors also have the students list the five people who have had the greatest influence on their values and discuss the significance of their choices.

In another section of the book, the authors have the students list *commandments,* the ten commandments (or basic values) of their family, the ten commandments of their school, the ten commandments of their peers, the ten commandments by which their teachers seem to live, the ten commandments by which they choose to live. Each of those lists can easily provide starting points for writing.

Many teachers find journals to be a useful place for students to jot down ideas and thoughts that can then grow into full-fledged writing projects. Some teachers use journals for daily writing—freewriting—while others use the journal less frequently. We pass out a sheet at the beginning of the term with suggestions for journal writing topics:

Profiles and portraits. Short sketches of friends, enemies, family members, public figures.

Satire. Short pieces poking fun at dorm or cafeteria food, school regulations, clothing fads, school organizations.

Opinion pieces. Thoughts about school, town, state, or national issues.

Advertisements. Satires or real ads for products, ideas, beliefs, or even people.

Metaphors. New words and images for old ideas. "As pretty as _____." "A sunrise like _____." "Ugly as _____." "Quick as _____." "Sly as _____."

Confessions. Real or imaginary.

Poems. Limericks, light verse, concrete poetry, haiku.

Observations and studies. An old woman at the coffee shop; a tree blooming outside your window; a baby eating an ice cream cone; an ant struggling with a crumb; a student studying in the library.

Sense impressions. Descriptions of the sound of wind, the feel of corduroy, the taste and feel of ice cream, the odor of tar or gasoline, the feel of rain, the sound of traffic.

Dialogue. Conversations as they've been heard or conversations made up in the writer's head.

We often open class with a brief five or ten minute writing period—a warm-up time—with students writing in journals. Often simply writing one of the categories on the board will be enough to spark a flow. Later, as we review the journals, we often point out passages or ideas that we think can be treated at greater length in a paper.

We have freely borrowed ideas from Bill Zavatsky and Ron Padgett's *Whole Word Catalogue II* (1975), a book principally useful for elementary school teachers, but one whose writing warm-ups work with students at any age level. Our adaptation of their suggestions includes:

The Most Amazing Thing. Encourage students to use their imaginations to make up the wildest, most incredible scene or person that they can. Then have them write about the most amazing real thing (not something from movies or TV) that they have actually seen. Other variations can include: the most horrible thing, the most beautiful thing, the most frightening thing.

Challenge Verse. Give students the last line of a story and have them write the story that ends with that line: "So I spit in his eye and walked away." "But no matter what I did, the red spot wouldn't come off." "The sun set in a purple haze."

Found Poems. Have students look for catchy or unusual or quaint passages
in books, magazines, and newspapers and write them out
in a form that suggests
    they might even be
      poems.

Explositions. Students describe what happens when something explodes:
popcorn, an oil tank, a runner.

These informal writing activities can be viewed like dance warm-ups or
athletic limbering up exercises. The purpose is to get the juices flowing, to
generate and discover ideas, to experiement with new words, to let off steam,
to expand awareness. They can be done as part of journal writing or simply
as a short activity at the beginning of the class. Such writings should not be
graded or evaluated for correctness and usage. However, we often encourage
students to share their writings, or we collect a batch of papers and read
several anonymously on the spur of the moment.

During the first several days of class we also encourage students to talk
about themselves and their backgrounds. In the schools, of course, many
students already know one another from previous classes, but in college (and
in many large schools), students need to learn who their classmates are and
what is interesting about them.

One activity we have used with success is to have the students bring to
class an object that says something important about them or symbolizes
them in an important way. In class we direct conversation around the room
and have each person show the object and describe its significance. Students
bring in class rings, stuffed animals, posters, basketballs, baseballs, trophies,
flowers, photographs, postcards, and so on. While we use this principally
as a discussion activity, we also remind students that behind each object
is at least one and perhaps several stories that could be written.

We also use storytelling to help students learn more about each other. In
pairs, students will tell one another significant stories about themselves,
stories they think expose their character or reveal something about them.
The person listening to the story then chooses one he or she finds appealing
and writes it up for sharing with the rest of the class. In this way, a person is
able to tell a story and see it translated into print without actually having to
take full responsibility for the writing.

An admittedly wacky variation on the same activity has the students write
fictional biographies of one another. We have the students pair with another
person they do not know and—strictly on the basis of impressions—write a
biography, making it as crazy and imaginative as possible. The biographies
are read aloud to the class for laughs; then the biographee describes who, in

fact, he or she is. The activity sets a light, relaxed tone for the class, and the biographies, though fictional, tell a surprising amount about how people perceive each other.

These kinds of early classroom experiences often set the tone for the entire course. It is valuable to encourage helpfulness and appreciation of individuals, while inviting students to analyze and write about personal experiences.

EXPLORING THE SELF

All good writing is personal, for one cannot write well about something that one does not know about or care about. We emphasize writing about the self in the early phases of our courses for a variety of reasons. For young writers, in particular, the exploration of experiences, fantasies, dreams, nightmares, and values helps people gain perspective on their past, helps them understand themselves, and helps them reflect on who they are. In addition, writing about personal experience is something students can do successfully and can enjoy sharing with an audience.

Initially, students may feel that nothing in their experience is significant enough or interesting enough to write about. But the kinds of inventories described in the previous section ought to have given them a sense that the teacher and fellow classmates value their stories and ideas. In addition, we prime the pump by offering some of the following ideas as options.

Choose an experience, event, or period in your life that had some significance for you. Consider one of the following possibilities:

An experience in your life when you were the center of attention—the star, the hero, a winner.

An incident in your life when you felt failure, disappointment, or embarrassment.

An event or experience in which you learned something important about yourself or other people. (Try to describe the incident so the reader experiences what you felt and you do not have to tack on a "moral.")

A tragic event in your life, or an incident that caused you sadness or pain.

An experience or period in which you felt angry, hostile, or alienated.

Something you did that you were sorry about later.

A positive relationship with someone—another person your age, a teacher, an important adult, your first love, your best friend.

A relationship in which you felt hurt, betrayed, misled, or undermined.

Those topics invite first person narrative, but we also suggest to students that they can explore their personal experiences in other discourse modes. Thus we offer some of these topics as alternatives:

Write a letter to an unborn child of yours describing an experience that holds great significance for you.

Write a letter (that you may wish *not* to mail) to your parents describing an experience you have had that you've never shared with them because you were too embarrassed or were afraid of their reaction.

Write a fictionalized account of one of your own experiences, turning it into a short story that happened to somebody else.

Write about one of your own experiences from the point of view of someone else who was there at the time: your friend, a parent, a brother or sister, your enemy.

After students have had an opportunity to look over the list of writing ideas, we ask if anyone knows what he/she is going to write about. For some students, an idea springs to mind just as soon as you mention a few possibilities; for others the list triggers ideas other than those you have described. The students who have ideas may describe for the rest of the class what they think they might write about, thus generating some prewriting discussion. This provides the teacher with an opportunity to approach the subject of structure—obliquely—by encouraging the students to keep focus on a single event or happening. It is easy for students to get so involved in the assignment that they present a catalogue of events, instead of a single episode.

The topics we have listed above actually provide material for a series of activities, not just one. Ordinarily we offer students a choice of, say, five or six topics at a time, lest they be overwhelmed. Usually every student in the class will find several events to write about, and we linger at this phase, encouraging students to mine their experience carefully.

When the class seems ready, we move a bit deeper into their inner worlds, into personal hopes and fears, daydreams, fantasies, and nightmares. Drawing on Miller and Judy's *Writing in Reality* (1978), we suggest that students write about the pictures and events of their subconscious by suggesting the following possibilities:

Write about a recurring dream or nightmare. Tell it as a story, then write an interpretation of it.

Create an imaginary dream for yourself. If you were in charge of composing your own dreams, what scenario would you sketch out?

Write about one of your dreams as a play.

Everybody daydreams—write down one of yours.

To get students started on these topics, we often have them do a stream of consciousness writing in which they explore the images of their fantasies.

We tell them to write whatever they can remember about their dreams and nightmares, describing them in running narrative form or through lists of pictures, scenes, and images. Some people don't remember dreams and nightmares and draw on their daydreams. After this kind of warm-up, they settle on a topic and write about it in detail.

Some teachers have criticized these topics as both frivolous and as an invasion of the students' privacy. We believe that preserving students' privacy is important, and we offer the students the option of not sharing these papers with their classmates. However, we have in the past had few takers of that option, and, in fact, the dreams and nightmares paper is one of our best activities for promoting class discussion. Further, it evokes good writing; dreams and nightmares are so close to the self, so important to the writer, and so vivid that this energy is carried over into their writing.

Other topics that encourage writers to explore the self center on the roles people see themselves playing and on the personalities they choose to project to others. (These topics, of course, are closely related to the rhetorical concept of voice.) The writing is somewhat more abstract than the previous topics, asking for the students to make abstractions about roles and personalities. Where the dreams paper invites sensory description by its very nature, roles are often perceived as abstractions: I am a leader/follower/star/satellite.

In preparing students to write, the teacher needs to (1) help students make valid generalizations drawing on previous experiences as the basis for those generalizations and (2) show students how to relate significant and apt examples to their generalizations.

Among the topics we suggest are:

Write a paper describing yourself as you see you and as another person might see you (your mother, your grandmother, your best friend, your chemistry professor, your enemy, your sweetheart). Compare these pictures of yourself.

Choose a time when you had to do something that went against your grain, that required you to do something you really didn't want to do. Describe the episode and your feelings during it.

Write two letters to two different people about an important event that happened to you or about an interesting or unusual idea that you have. Write the letters to people with different values and beliefs: a priest, your enemy, an imaginary being, a person who lived in the past, a movie star.

Write about a time when you were told two versions of the same story. In retelling this event, try to make it clear how your personality changed as you told the two tales.

Begin an essay with the sentence, "I am not the person people think I am."

Yet another series of writing topics exploring the self centers on students' looking into their own futures. We introduce these topics by saying:

Consider the kind of person you are, the kind of person you want to be, your goals and aims, your ideas about how you will achieve what you want and how you will make your mark. Consider the ways in which you are unique and creative and/or how you want to develop your own uniqueness and creativity. Consider how you plan to say "I am" to the world. Some of the following statements might trigger ideas for your paper:

Although I know the kind of person I want to be, I often feel pressure to be something else, to be someone else.

There are some ways in which I am really creative and I feel I will be able to make a positive contribution to those with whom I live and work.

I am torn about the kind of person I want to be. Some of my values, goals, and beliefs seem to be in conflict with one another.

As I mature, I am becoming more and more the kind of person I want to be. I am concentrating on some particularly important areas of my development.

There are some things about myself that I don't like. In the next few years I would like to change some aspects of my character or personality.

By the time I am twenty-five (forty/sixty-five) I plan to be . . .

Those who know me recognize how I make my statement: "I am."

Some of these topics lead to papers in which students make generalizations about themselves; others (like the last two) lead to papers that are scenarios of future lives. For both types of papers, the teacher needs to become involved in helping the students be specific and concrete, *discouraging* them from making broad abstractions about, say *wealth* or *motherhood* or *success*. They should not lose the skill, developed earlier, of writing about themselves with focus and specificity.

The reader will note that the topics described in this section, we have *not* specified external audiences beyond the classroom. In general, personal writing of this sort is meant for the writer alone, for the teacher (who functions as a trusted adult), or for a few close friends and classmates. As students move toward exploring relations with others, the circle of audiences can be expanded as well.

ONESELF AND OTHERS

Character sketches, analyses of family, friends, and associates, tributes to and condemnations of people, and pieces written from the point of view of others create opportunities for students to extend the range of their writing abilities by seeing how others tick and understanding how others affect them.

Character sketches focusing on description of people's physical and personality traits are a good starting point for writing about others. A good in-class assignment is to have students write a description of a person—perhaps someone in the class—concentrating on the physical details of the person alone. Or you might have students observe a stranger (in a gift shop, at a clothing store) and write a description. Students can see that physical traits, gestures, facial expression, and language can reflect the character traits of the person they are describing.

Once students have done a basic physical description, possibly as a warm-up activity, they can move into some of the following topics:

Describe someone you dislike without directly telling the readers you dislike the person. Focus on physical descriptions or descriptions of actions to communicate your viewpoint.

Describe a person about whom you had a change of opinion—someone you first disliked and then grew to like or the other way around. Describe the behavior that led to the change.

Describe an enemy in a way that will make your readers like him or her.

Describe someone who is a mystery to you. Try to dramatize the behavior that you don't understand.

Write a dialogue between you and an enemy or between you and a friend.

Where character sketches emphasize appearance and behavior for their own sake, analysis or interpretation of a people not only describes them but helps the reader understand why the people act as they do. Students might enjoy analyzing a friend, roomate, teacher, administrator, sibling, or parent. It is important that the writers try to view their topic in some depth, not focusing solely on superficial traits or characterists. A list of questions can help students see their subject in more detail:

What facts do I know about this person's life?

What personality qualities do I like least about this person?

What traits do I like best?

What are this person's dominant physical traits?

Who is this person most like? Most unlike?

Who are his or her friends? Enemies? Why?

How has this person changed during the time I have known him or her?

What are the person's goals and values?

How do I feel when I'm around this person?

Sometimes students can answer questions or discuss in detail the qualities and traits that bring the person to life, but then have difficulty getting this down on paper. It is important to continue to emphasize the necessity for concrete pictures, scenes, details, and sensory data as the basis for the analysis.

Students seem to have difficulty, too, in writing tributes or condemnations. Because their feelings are so strong about a person, they have a tendency to believe that others view the subject in the same way. In addition, they rely on abstractions about the person: *stupid, ugly, loud, insensitive, boring, wild;* or *beautiful, kind, helpful, intelligent, funny, creative.* When such abstractions emerge in their papers, ask the students to write or describe the bases on which they came to their conclusions. Have them write illustrations, examples, scenes, and episodes that provide evidence for each abstraction.

Writing from another person's point of view helps students describe more fully than they do ordinarily, because they are less likely to assume so much, to take things for granted. Moreover, students are intrigued by other people's viewpoints and experiences and enjoy "getting into somebody else's skin." Students find the experience more mind stretching if they choose someone who is quite different from them, someone whose experiences and beliefs are very unlike the writer's. For example, students can write:

About an argument they had with a friend, taking the point of view of the adversary.

A description of themselves from the point of view of their enemy.

A journal or diary entry by someone much older, much younger, or of the opposite sex.

Short stories from the point of view of someone else.

Letters, monologues, and stream of consciousness papers give students the opportunity to identify and reproduce the ideas and inner emotions of other people. Thus the journal can be brought into play and students can practice perceiving from someone else's point of view before plunging into paper writing.

Perhaps the most useful form for learning about the feelings and emotions of others and how to portray them is *drama.* Playwriting is popular with students of almost all ages, and it is, in its way, a complete discourse form, encouraging the writer to produce a rich mix of writing types. Too, when writers must describe the words and gestures of a character in order to make that character come to life, they must think carefully about physical details and conversations.

Sometimes dramas can be true to life. Students can recreate scenes they have seen "in nature":

A quarrel between lovers or friends.

A stranger asking directions from somebody.

A dispute between a bus driver/shopkeeper/restauranteur about prices or change.

A confrontation between a student and a teacher.

But the whole world of fictional drama is open to students as well. They can create one-act plays, television scripts, radio plays, and scripts for reader's theater presentations. Creating plays also creates a natural demand for presentation and audiences, providing an opportunity for the teacher to extend the range of people reading and/or reacting to students' work. Initially, performances may be restricted to the class where the play has been written, but they may easily and quickly be extended to other classes, the whole school or campus groups, and even to the community. (See also Chapter 6, which discusses audiences for student writing.)

EXPLORING ISSUES, PROBLEMS, AND VALUES

As we have said previously, writing is not only a way of expressing what one knows; it is also a means for discovering what you know and learning things you did not know. Some knowledge is acquired by reading books and taking courses, but much is learned by observing the world and carefully watching its happenings. As they become more confident in their ability to describe themselves and others, we encourage students to begin analyzing their world: the *environments* (the groups, institutions, media, organizations) that shape their lives and the systems of *values* and *beliefs* (educational, religious, social, intellectual) by which they live.

Many young writers have not had opportunities to think consciously about such matters, and their first writings tend to be overgeneralized, abstract, and unconvincing. They often recite values that they have heard and regard institutions as set and predetermined; they tend not to be analytical or critical about their environment.

We encourage students to write on issues and beliefs that affect them directly, that they know about firsthand. Religious beliefs, television programming, the school or college curriculum, the school paper, smoking and drinking, sexual relationships, young people's rights, and other topics close to home provide ample material for the students to write about with vigor. Further, students need to be helped to draw on their experiences—both first and secondhand—and to recognize the complexity of the issues that may be involved. It is important for students to go through the writing process carefully, taking as much time as needed to marshall ideas, consider an audience, plan, draft, and revise.

On controversial issues, for example, there is nothing like class discussion as a prewriting activity to help students clarify their thinking. Though free-for-all arguments with everyone shouting are no help, discussions in which people present strongly different views are useful and stimulating. In this kind of discussion the teacher needs to encourage students to relate specific examples and incidents that led them to their opinions. (The early work in writing about personal experience and about other people comes into play here.)

Discussion of audience is appropriate as part of the prewriting discussion as well. On some issues—say, rights for young adults—students in a class may be of one mind, so that their papers, if restricted to the class as audience, would merely be preaching to the converted. Then, it is appropriate for the teacher to consider ways of enlarging the range of audiences to include others—those not converted. (Again, see Chapter 6 and its discussion of audiences outside the classroom.) Students need to consider some of the following kinds of questions:

Who will my readers for this paper be? How many of them already share my beliefs or my view of the solution? How many don't?

What experiences of mine led me to my beliefs?

How can I share or describe those experiences precisely for others (without boring them)?

What counterarguments are they likely to present?

What are my answers to those arguments?

In discussing revision (Chapter 5) we will describe the "devil's advocate" response as a way of helping students generate strong arguments and position statements. That technique is appropriate here, both as a kind of prewriting discussion and in the evaluation and assessment of rough drafts by young writers and their peers.

We encourage our students to consider the various forms that these kinds of papers can take. If they are describing the beliefs by which they live, for example, we suggest that they consider putting their ideas into a letter, possibly a letter to a friend, a parent, or a person they know would disagree with them. Sometimes humorous pieces, including satire, can be a useful mode of discussion. Our students have woven their beliefs into forms as diverse as essays, editorials, short stories, plays, and even poems.

As part of coming to understand their beliefs and values, we have our students examine some of the cultural phenomena and the institutions that strongly affect their lives. They may write a paper about a movie (or the current crop of movies), a television program (or the state of video), a musical or theatrical event, or a magazine or magazine article. They may also examine physical structures and institutions: shopping malls, cafeterias, bars, the football stadium, a church, a public gathering place.

In these papers, students should aim to see below the surface structure, below the appearances, to perceive how the phenomenon may be influencing their lives. We provide our students with a list of questions to help guide them in their thinking:

What are the important aspects of the subject you are analyzing? What are its outstanding traits or qualities? What are its positive qualities? Its negative ones?

What does it look like, sound like, feel like, or taste like? (Write down very specific observations so you can base your writing in concrete detail.)

What effect does your subject have on you? Does it please you? Stimulate you? Anger you? Irritate you? Frustrate you? Sadden you? Make you laugh or cry?

What effect does your subject have on other people?

How does your subject fit into the larger environment in which we all live?

What are its causes? What made it become what it is?

What are its long-range effects? What it will be like twenty, thirty, or sixty years from now?

It is often useful to have students engage in listmaking with this kind of topic, jotting down answers to the questions above to provide a set of specific observations that will be woven into the paper. Often we find that in answering the questions the students discover parts, aspects, or effects of their subject they had not perceived or understood before. As a useful prewriting activity, you may want to take the class through common analysis of a single topic, say the existence of the local Burger Qwik fast food restaurant, to see how the questions provide them with material for writing.

Once again we invite our students to move beyond the mode of the essay and to select unusual or distinct points of view. Our students have written papers analyzing football from the point of view of a man unfamiliar with the game, describing a college bar from the point of view of a parent, showing what life would be like without the existence of television, and explaining through a poem the impact of electricity on humankind.

INVESTIGATING/PROBING/RESEARCHING

We believe that writing about something is a good way to learn, to get control over information and to integrate that information into one's own ideas and thoughts. The purpose of the traditional research paper, according to many of its proponents, is to do just that. Yet, as it is commonly taught to upper level high schoolers and to college freshmen, the research paper is, to our minds, a less than useful exercise. Why? We see several flaws in the kind of research assignment conventionally offered.

1. The research paper is isolated from other learning in a course. It does not grow out of ideas, issues, or information that has been the subject of study in the course. Topics are often picked out of the air by the students or selected from a laundry list offered by the teacher. Thus the topic exists in a vacuum.

2. In the teaching of the research paper there is an overemphasis on form and a lack of concern for the development of thoughts and ideas. Too often it is taught principally as a way of forcing students to learn how to use the library and how to use proper footnote and bibliographic forms.

3. The research paper overemphasizes one kind of research—library research—at the expense of other modes of learning such as interviewing and actual laboratory research. The net effect is that most student written research papers are not discovery experiences at all, but are merely a regurgitation of previously published material. In the process, the research paper distorts the concept of research and presents a peculiar picture of the researcher as someone who writes for encyclopedias.

4. Research paper writing seldom follows the steps of the composing process. Because of the length of time required to do a paper, teachers tend to assign them for outside-of-class work. There is no prewriting discussion of ideas and audiences, no sharing of drafts, little in-class discussion of needed revisions. Thus the research paper may undercut or militate against the workshop approach we have advocated throughout this book.

But we also agree that students must learn research skills and, for the college bound at least, they need to know something of the formalities of preparing and submitting papers. How, then, can research and research writing be made a sensible, practical activity for school and college writing courses?

At this point the reader, knowing the principles we have espoused in the book and seeing the examples of assignments earlier in this chapter, could suggest a number of possible approaches.

Ours center on having students write on topics of their own choosing, finding information and resources from many sources, writing for audiences that can be genuinely informed by the paper, and using a workshop approach to guide the students through all stages of research and writing. We should add, too, that we do not think that research writing must result in long papers or heavily documented ones. Sometimes it may simply involve writing up an interview or a personal experience. Other times it may grow from reading a novel, several short stories, and some magazines (not just an encyclopedia). In our use of the term, the "research paper" becomes very broad. It may be essay or poem or play as well as a formal, documented term paper.

Students' research should be based on their own questions and their own concerns. Research into general or abstract topics is not likely to be successful unless the students have some prior experience or deep curiosity about the area.

The best topics are those related to the students' families, friends, schools, or communities. Histories of families, family trees, biographies of famous or infamous ancestors, and family apocyphal stories might interest some students. What professions seem to dominate in your family? How do various members of your family (aunts, uncles, grandparents, cousins) define success? What roles do women play in your family? What religious traditions and social customs have survived in your family? These family-oriented topics call chiefly for interviews as a method of research, but often background readings—library research—are appropriate, too.

The students' own age group can provide a solid base for research, and not simply narcissistic investigation of the self. What's happening to your body *now*? (A research question that is of interest to young or old.) What are the interests, values, mores of your peer group? Where do they come from? What do you and your peers think important in the world? Where do they stand as a group on key issues of the day? What has made you and your group the way you are? For historical research, the teacher can even have students investigate their peer group and its values of twenty-five, fifty, or one hundred years ago. What did teenagers do, think, and believe in the middle of the nineteenth century? What was college life like then?

School history, organizations, activities, and administrative policies can be the basis for research. In larger schools, students may not know about how concerts and lectures are planned and executed, how cafeteria or dorm food is purchased and prepared, how sororities and clubs function, how school rules and policies are developed. Often, with involvement of the administration, such research papers can serve a useful function in school planning, thus providing a real audience for the student writer.

The community offers myriad institutions and activities to explore. Community history, for example, can be written on everything from policies to buildings. Where did the old city hall come from? Who designed it? What were the first buildings in our town? Why is the town located here? What provided its early financial base? How has the financial base shifted over the years? What are the principal professions/lifestyles/religions? What is the future of the town? Is it changing? growing? decaying?

Students can investigate specific groups or functions in the community: firefighters, police officers, the aging, daycare centers, museums, the performing arts, food services. What makes them operate and continue to grow? What is their future?

The world of popular culture is also a basis for exploration by young people, touching on the world beyond school and community but having close ties to the students themselves. One research unit we have taught has students work in groups to investigate a theme of popular culture that appears throughout the media. Students explore such areas and topics as: The American Dream (or Nightmare), Heroes and Heroines in the Media, The Sports Craze, The Search for Beauty, Images of Women, Images of Childhood, Images of Young Adults, Spiritualism and the Occult, Love and Marriage, Hate and Divorce. Students are not limited to these topics, and they can choose a movement or value that seems to pervade American life and media presentations. Each member of the group reads about and conducts research into aspects of the topic individually. Then the groups get together to share information and answers to questions, with the group planning leading to presentations back to the class as a whole. Each student takes responsibility for writing one portion of the presentation, but the group as a whole helps to guide individual writers.

A common element running through these projects is that research is conducted in many different ways. We encourage our students to use books and periodicals (and, yes, we give them a brief introduction to library skills), but we emphasize that research questions can be answered through letters, phone calls, interviews, and surveys. We also encourage students to look for publications *not* in the library: the yellow pages, public service guides, government pamphlets, brochures published by manufacturers and business people.

We encourage writers to draw on the electronic media as well, for we prefer to *use* the media, not fight them. We emphasize that television, radio, films, and records contain important current information, particularly as a reflection of popular culture, and we place value on *interpretive* data gathering, in which the students make judgments about the meanings of ideas presented through the media.

Running through our research projects is the assumption that research papers need not be dry, dull, rehashed information collected from dusty library books. Research should involve the interaction of the mind of the writer with the data he or she finds. It should involve active observation, questioning, thinking, reading, and discussion with others.

Students should maintain their personal voices when they write research and not drift off into academese. Moreover, they need not limit the results of their research to the term paper. They can write stories, dialogues, dramas, satires, editorials, letters, or newspaper and magazine articles to communicate the knowledge they have gained.

The audience for research writing ought to be a real one, so we encourage students to select subjects that others may be interested in reading about, audiences that range from relatives excited about a family tree to a school administrator taking interest in proposed student government rearrangement. Indeed, actual publication may be possible for some student papers. Local newspapers and specialty magazines seek new perspectives on everything from campus life to the views of young people on sex, and they may welcome submission of well written student papers.

ADAPTING WRITING ACTIVITIES

In this chapter we have presented a broad range of writing activities that we have experimented with or observed in our school and college teaching. We do not assume that these topics can be lifted directly from the book and plugged into any teaching situation with success. Some of these topics are better suited to younger writers than to older ones; others touch on subjects that are taboo at various school levels. We are certain that we have neglected some areas that are important to the reader and possibly overstressed others.

The point of the chapter is to provide some starting points and some models for the reader to use in evolving his or her own set of writing activities for particular students. Further, there is always the delicate balance between providing students with opportunities to write on a variety of subjects and giving them a surfeit of possibilities. Students should be encouraged to stretch their thinking and writing abilities, not allowed to become dependent on teacher-supplied topics or gimmicks. Students who are certain of their writing ability may be eager to choose their own topics, while less confident writers may need some—but not too much—guidance. The goal of the course should be to help students develop independence in deciding what it is they want to say and to whom they want to say it. The teacher of writing, while providing stimulation through writing ideas, should be equally concerned with encouraging students to design writing activities of their own.

CHAPTER 4

INTERDISCIPLINARY WRITING

The title for this chapter covers an unusually large area of the writing curriculum. It is intended to represent two closely related concepts: The first of these goes under the catch phrase "writing across the curriculum," suggesting that composition is a school- or college-wide concern, not just the domain of English teachers. The second deals with the content of writing programs and students' writings, presenting the view that composition is naturally and fundamentally interdisciplinary, touching on and probing into any and all subjects. This chapter is placed here because it is a natural extension of the material on writing activities presented in the previous chapter (in particular, the discussion of investigating/probing/researching). We will treat "assignment making" as it can take place with an interdisciplinary focus within English classes and as it ought, ideally, to happen throughout the school or college curriculum.

The idea of interdisciplinary writing is not new. As far back as the nineteenth century educators argued that to be taught successfully, composition had to be a concern of all teachers, that students would not grow as writers unless all teachers took responsibility for their literacy education (National Education Association, 1893). It has surfaced as a curriculum concern throughout the twentieth century, most recently in the "language across the curriculum" policy statements of our colleagues in Great Britain, Australia, and Canada (Britton, et al., 1975; Walshe, 1979; Styles and Cavanagh, 1980).

However, despite agreement among theorists that interdisciplinary programs are important, it is clear that colleagues in school and college subject matter departments have not been eager to take up the teaching of writing along with everything else. By and large they expect that the English faculty will take care of writing (by which they seem to mean "grammar") so that the students in their classes will be able to write flawlessly (or at least competently) on exams and papers. "If only the English people would do a better job," the refrain goes, "then I could get on with my work."

The reluctance of subject matter people to join in the quest for writing excellence is, perhaps, understandable. In the first place, they're extremely busy themselves, struggling to cover their own areas within the restrictions imposed by short terms, quarters, and semesters. There doesn't seem to be time for writing. In the second place, they haven't been trained to teach writing; most of them have no more writing experience than their training in freshman college composition few or many years ago. Lastly, they are often intimidated by language themselves, feeling self-conscious about their usage, doubtful of their own abilities as writers.

At the same time, the great amount of public attention focused on the teaching of writing these days has obviously attracted the interest of some teachers in other disciplines. We find that our graduate writing workshops for teachers now regularly include a few "outsiders": a biology teacher, a history teacher or two, even art and music teachers. These people come to us with a common concern: "I know my students write poorly and I want to do something about it." Although we do not anticipate that every subject teacher will be willing to take up the cause of writing, it seems clear to us that at no time has there been greater potential for development of interdisciplinary writing programs. Further, one hears or reads of many pilot programs being launched in schools and colleges across the country. (See, for example, *The National Writing Project Network Newsletter.*)

One sign of the new interest in subject matter writing is the radical suggestion made by some that writing be taken away from English faculties and turned over to the subject teachers. Here, for example, three professors of Engineering at the University of Michigan, J. C. Mathes, Dwight W. Stevenson, and Peter Klaver (1979), argue the case for removing technical writing from the hands of English professors:

> In the past, English departments have not usually favored technical writing. Indeed, they have not been enthusiastic about Freshman Composition, their traditional bread-and-butter course. But times have now changed. Because of declining enrollments, many English departments are inaugurating technical writing programs and courses.
>
> Engineering educators, however, must be wary of entrusting technical writing to English departments. First, English departments tend to view technical writing in terms of their traditional goals [training literary specialists, not scientists or engineers]. Second, some of the basic writing principles taught in English Composition courses are antithetical to the basic principles of technical writing. Third, most professors of English are trained to teach literature, not composition. (p. 5)

To many of these points, we say "touché." The professors' thrusts are on target; their blades are sharp; they easily draw English teachers' blood. We suspect, too, that a good many school subject teachers could make analogous charges about junior and high school writing programs and draw blood there.

Granting that English departments have been negligent in teaching subject matter writing (and have been reluctant to teach even basic writing in their own discipline), we have to disagree with Mathes, Stevenson, and Klaver on a key point: that the principles of English composition are "antithetical" to the concepts taught in technical writing programs. In fact, it is on that point of debate that we think the basis for statements of policy and program on writing across the curriculum can be developed.

By "antithetical," the three professors explain, they mean:

> *The principles taught in English composition derive from classical rhetoric, from the literary tradition, and from such humanistic educational objectives as self awareness.* (p. 6)

In technical writing, they imply, such principles have no place, since tech writing emphasizes objectivity, impartiality, and the unadorned presentation of basic material.

But neither classical nor contemporary rhetoric opposes those qualities in writing. Rather, as we have shown in Chapter 1, writing teachers are agreed that all writing must be taught as process, that writing must be authentic, and, most important, that writing is a mode of learning as well as a means of communication. Those principles, we believe, apply to subject matter writing as well as "English" writing—to technical writing, scientific writing, historical writing as well as to writing about literature or human experience.

We quarrel with the assumption that technical (and other scientific or scholarly writing) must be cold and objective, that it does not reflect an author's personal experience and "self awareness." We object to the principles in a college textbook, *The Technician as Writer*, written by two of the three same professors and another colleague (Brunner, Mathes, and Stevenson, 1980), that puts all of its effort into teaching the forms of technical writing, belying a title that implies a concern for the writer as well as the subject matter and structure of writing.

The central hypothesis of this chapter is that the needs of student writers in English and other classes coincide, and that both English and subject teachers can successfully teach interdisciplinary writing, each from his or her own perspective. Ideally, we would like to see the evolution of writing programs where responsibility is shared by all members of the faculty. In reality, it seems probable that a compromise situation will develop in most schools and colleges, with some (but not all) English faculty being concerned with subject matter writing and with some (but not all) instructors in the disciplines providing solid help to the students who have to write in their courses.

STEPS TOWARD A SCHOOL-WIDE WRITING PROGRAM

In this section we will suggest five steps or projects that can be undertaken by school and college faculties to develop interdisciplinary writing programs. We will begin "at home," suggesting that English faculty members should do much more to include disciplinary concerns in their writing programs. Then we will move toward the development of faculty-wide understanding about the nature of the writing process and suggest how joint or team efforts can develop. Finally, we will enter into a discussion of how specific interdisciplinary writing projects can be developed in either English or subject matter courses.

1. *Extend the dimensions of writing in English classes.* In Chapter 3 we suggested that topics for composition ought to be as broad and diverse as possible, covering a great many discourse modes and subject areas. Those subjects for writing ought to include other disciplines as well. Too often "English" is where one writes about literature alone. (We suspect this may, in part, be the source of the complaint by Mathes, Stevenson, and Klaver.) Alternatively, in writing classes students may grapple with issues of a pseudo-philosophical or political nature. They don't, in English, write very often about the solid content of other disciplines.

We have found that in our own teaching, opening up subject matter possibilities brings about a good response from many students who are traditionally nonwriters. To prime the pump, we spend an hour scanning the subject catalogue at the library, jotting down topics that seem to us intriguing: *arctic expeditions, brewing, cacti, child abuse, food synthesis, . . . X rays, Yucatan, zoology.* Each of these topics, we explain to the class, is the starting point for a good writing project, and we encourage students to explore their own subject matter interests, perhaps creating an alphabetical list of their own.

To show how such subjects can be developed, we can draw on the work of Frank Talbott (1980), a fifth grade teacher in Texas, who explains that for years he has had his students do creative writing in a variety of subject areas:

Social studies. Writing about imaginary countries; writing first person accounts of what it might have been like in the early American settlements.

Science. Writing science fiction; writing reports and discussions of in-class experiments.

Mathematics. Exploring life on a hypothetical two-dimensional planet, flat as a sheet of paper.

Health. Describing "The Most Unsafe House in the City" and telling how it might be improved.

It is important to stress that the English teacher who assigns these topics (or virtually any discipline-oriented topic) need not personally be a subject matter expert. That is, one does not have to know all about cyclotrons or amino acid structure or Russian history in order to encourage students to write about them. Nor must the English teacher necessarily know a great deal about the conventions of form and style used in the disciplines for formal research papers. In most cases, the subject papers students write in schools and colleges do not resemble formal research writing anyway; instead, the student is presenting information in popular style for an audience of nonspecialists: his or her classmates and the teacher. Thus the teacher can judge or edit the writing according to the standards for any good prose: clarity, focus, appropriateness, and so on.

The English interdisciplinary program should, however, be backed up by resources, and thus we suggest as a corollary:

1a. *Extend the dimensions of reading in English classes.* It seems to us that English teachers have been negligent in not drawing on the fullest possible range of reading materials for their classes. Too often they have been concerned only with literature—chiefly British and American. In the past two decades some teachers have extended this range, including world literature, ethnic literature, and the literature of popular and folk culture in their classes. But they have neglected rich resources in fiction and nonfiction that touch on interdisciplinary concerns. As an exercise in our young adult literature courses for prospective teachers, we have our students go to a paperback bookstore to look for titles that aren't ordinarily used in English classes. They find that the science section includes well-written books on topics from the origins of life to outer space travel, from beasts and bugs to ways of protecting the environment. The history section contains readable books on civil war history, naval history, the history of one's community or state. In the social science and psychology sections one can find everything from the popular self-help books to investigations of current social and economic issues. The math books cover topics from computer games to the use of pocket calculators. Nor do our students ignore the magazine sections, where they find good material that includes *Scientific American, American History, Old West, Science Digest,* and *Popular Psychology,* to name just a few of hundreds of good interdisciplinary publications.

Public school teachers know of the value of in-class libraries and can bring in these kinds of materials, purchasing them through the school budget or borrowing them from the library. Simply getting these books into the room provides a good starting point for interdisciplinary writing. Few college instructors have the luxury of a classroom library; rather, they need to alert students to the availability of such materials and encourage them to search the library for them.

Curiously, subject matter teachers tend not to draw on the popular or trade books in their areas, perhaps feeling that the books are not sufficiently complex in their treatment. Thus the English teacher will hear no outraged cry if he or she encourages the students to read them. Further, to our way of thinking, the popular books contain good, solid content in a highly readable form. Who would want to read about the origins of life in a dreary biology textbook when one could hear about it from the witty, articulate Isaac Asimov in a two hundred page paperback?

2. *Establish HELP! centers for students with subject matter writing problems.* We are disturbed by the number of remedial "laboratories" and "clinics" that are being established in schools and colleges in an attempt to solve the writing crisis. In our experience, remedial centers often heighten writing problems because of their stress on basics and drill. In one such center we visited—admittedly an extreme situation—students found themselves being assigned to "learning stations" named after parts of speech— the Verb Center, the Noun Place, the Adjective Clinic—where, presumably, individual faults were corrected.

We find the concept of remediation in writing an uncomfortable one that is also limited in usefulness. It implies that one can establish standards for writing that apply to all students regardless of their previous experience, present interests, and future plans. We don't think that such standards can be established, and thus the term "remedial" loses meaning. In its place, we substitute a concept that we call "the commitment to teach," which simply means that the teacher determines that he or she will, to borrow an ancient pedagogical slogan, "take the students where they are and move them to someplace new."

Further, we agree with Suzanne Jacobs (1974), director of the writing program at the University of Hawaii, who argues that there is really only one writing course a person needs to take—that is the course that is needed *now*. Few remedial centers offer help with the problems the student faces in day-to-day work. In fact, some centers *prohibit* the students from bringing course work into class. We suggest as an alternative, the HELP! center, dedicated to the proposition that any time a student needs or wants help with a particular writing assignment, he or she can get it. A HELP! center need not contain expensive skill labs, workbooks, or grammar worksheets. Rather, when students come to the center they should find tutors—paid faculty, paraprofessional aides, parent volunteers, or fellow students—who will provide them with support and guidance.

Faced with a writing assignment, the students might find a tutor who would:

Help them understand the precise nature of the assignment: what's being asked for, what needs to go into the paper to complete the assignment.

Discuss possible resources for the paper.

Review notes and rough outlines, offering suggestions and advice.

Help the writer get the first words down, overcoming writing blocks.

Critique rough drafts.

Assist with the final polishing and proofreading of the paper.

The tutor does not write the paper for the student. Nor is the tutor to be held responsible in any way for the grade the student earns. (Such restrictions and ground rules need to be made clear to the users of the center from the very beginning.) However, the tutor can obviously supply substantial help with all phases of the writing project, serving, in effect, as a writing process coach.

This is not the place to go into the details of organizing and staffing such a center. There is plenty of help available in the professional literature. (An excellent starting point is Nina Luban, Ann Matsuhashi, and Tom Rigstad, "One-to-One to Write: Establishing an Individual Conference Writing Place," 1978. Also see our comments on conferencing and centers in Chapter 7.) Our principal point, once again, is that the center should provice assistance with specific papers and be available to all students. It should not be perceived as a skills-and-drill lab used only by lower ability students. Everybody needs HELP!

3. *Hold all-faculty meetings to discuss the teaching and learning of language.* Thanks in large measure to coverage by the media, the general public and subject matter teachers have been misinformed about the teaching of writing. Typically, our colleges think that teaching writing is like teaching multiplication: One teaches the "fundamentals" (the times tables or grammar) and then applies them (doing math problems or writing papers). Further, subject teachers generally seem to have accepted the media's "language decay" theory that erroneously describes an absolute decline in literacy levels.

To remedy this state of misinformation, English departments should sponsor meetings and seminars for the rest of the faculty. English teachers can respond to questions from their colleagues about the strengths and weaknesses of student writers and, more important, describe what can and cannot be achieved within English composition classes. The English faculty can politely but firmly suggest that subject teachers must take some responsibility for preparing students for success in the reading and writing they assign.

At such meetings the topic of theme grading and "good" English will predictably come up. The English faculty might want to be forearmed with some sort of position statement on that issue. A publication of the Conference on College Composition and Communication (1974), "Students' 'Right' to Their Own Language," might provide a starting point for discussion.

Among the other topics that might be raised at such a meeting, we would suggest the following:

> What are the responsibilities of English departments to teach writing in other disciplines? Are they to be merely "service departments"? Can an English teacher reasonably be expected to prepare students for all writing assignments they face elsewhere?

> What kinds of writing are actually required in the subject matter courses? Do students write in history and science classes or do they simply fill in the blanks? What kinds of writing would the subject matter teachers like to assign if students wrote better?

> What are the characteristics of good writing in the disciplines? Which of the writing forms practiced by professionals—scholars—are appropriate for students? What are the characteristics of popular writing in the disciplines? How do these differ from formal or scholarly writing?

> How do the subject matter teachers themselves go about writing? What does their experience in writing have to contribute to our understanding of how young people write?

From this discussion might come specialized seminars or work parties involving the subject matter teachers who would like to probe further. Not all faculty members in a school or college will want to participate, but for those who do, the English department might organize some informative, enlightening sessions. These follow-up meetings might even develop a policy statement on the teaching of writing that could serve the entire school or college. (For one such statement, see the Ontario Ministry of Education's "Language Across the Curriculum: A Resource Document for Principals and Teachers," 1978.)

4. *Provide English department help for subject matter writing assignments.* Several years ago the Grosse Pointe, Michigan, public schools released an English teacher part time to serve as a writing consultant to subject teachers (Fox, 1976). Her task was to assist teachers in improving the quality of their writing assignments. Among the roles she found herself playing were:

> *a typing teacher helping kids compose at the typewriter; an office practice*

teacher demonstrating how to write letters based on scrawled comments in the margins of incoming letters; a notehand teacher developing research techniques in combination with notehand skills; an industrial co-op teacher helping students with job applications and resumes; a commercial foods teacher showing students how to write PA announcements for the coffee shop; a retailing teacher responding to student-prepared ads for the student store; a civics teacher assigning a career paper; an Age of Majority teacher diverting rebellion into letters to editors and congressmen; a geometry teacher assigning proofs written in paragraph form; a science teacher showing how to take notes from reading; a foreign language teacher illustrating English syntax; a teacher in any class teaching Jane and Johnny how to take notes from lectures, how to write an introduction, or how to write an answer to an essay question on a test.

(p. 39)

Of course few school districts or colleges can afford to assign a teacher to serve as consultant in this way, though the list of activities above ought to make it clear that such a system is highly desirable. A low cost alternative is for the English department to create an informal consultant or buddy system so that subject area teachers can seek ways of improving writing. Thus the science teacher, wanting to quiz some students about the nature of the DNA molecule, might learn from an English buddy that a successful assignment would have students to visualize themselves as being inside the spiral helix and to write about it from that point of view. The history teacher, concerned about having students understand the causes of the Civil War, might draw on the suggestion that students write letters from the point of view of Northern and Southern sympathizers. The driver education teacher could discover that a good way to help students understand the rules of the road is for them to attempt to write reasonable traffic regulations themselves.

In addition to strengthening relationships and adding enormously to good will toward English departments, the consultant system begins to lay the groundwork for possible interdisciplinary or team taught courses. Informal collaboration between the science and English teacher might lead to a course or unit in "Science Fact/Science Fiction." The historian and the English teacher might want to work up something on "The Literature and History of the Civil War." The driver ed and English teacher might even want to work literature and writing into the driver training course through an interdisciplinary unit on "Wheels."

5. *Have subject area teachers take responsibility for describing the writing processes and forms unique to their disciplines.* We've suggested that English faculty members can do more than they have in the past to teach interdisciplinary writing. But the English department cannot do the job completely, and English should not be reduced to being a service course,

merely preparing students for writing experiences elsewhere. No English teacher, not matter how well prepared or well meaning, can get students ready for any writing assignment they may eventually face in somebody else's class.

Each teacher has his or her own set of standards about what makes "good" writing, and it is clearly the responsibility of the teacher—English or subject area—to make those idiosyncratic expectations clear. Some teachers want to see the students display original thinking; others simply want to be apprised of the facts. Some teachers want tightly structured, point by point essays; others prefer a more casual arrangement of content and argument. If students are to succeed at writing assignments, the instructor must take responsibility for describing what he or she wants.

Further, subject teachers are in the best position to present the forms and processes of writing in the disciplines. And it is here that all teachers can overcome the traditional schism between subject area and English teachers, the barrier alluded to by Stevenson, Mathes, and Klaver. When subject area writing is taught—either by English or subject specialists—it is too often taught as mastery of form rather than process. That is, the Technical Writing course consists of introducing students to the specific formal constraints of technical reports and papers. Business Writing seems to be an introduction to sundry kinds of forms and letters used in the commercial world. Science Writing is a presentation of the conventions of style and footnote form in the principal scientific journals. In such courses, the writing process and its concern for gathering and shaping materials for a specific audience seems forgotten.

We are persuaded that students can write subject papers much more effectively if they understand how the discipline evolved and how writing is interwoven with the transactions of the discipline. For instance, the form of the technical report didn't just "happen"; it evolved as a result of engineers' specific needs to get their findings—their research—down on paper in a compact, comprehensible form. History has its particular processes of discovery, and these are reflected in the form and style of history articles and books. Even driver training—to return to an example we used earlier—can be seen to have its written forms (the rules of the road) that were derived from a writing process (someone studied a traffic problem and tried to control it through language).

To explore this idea, one of us had a college class of non-English majors study the writing forms and processes of their major disciplines. The students interviewed professors and reviewed papers and exams they themselves had previously written. They raised the question, "How do ideas in my major area find their way into language?" Then they reported back to class.

A chemistry major showed how a professor's work in the laboratory—something to do with enzyme chemistry—was refined and developed into a theory, tested through experimentation, presented as a speech at a major convention, and eventually published as a paper in the *Journal of the American Chemical Society*. A history major told how a history professor drew on primary and secondary sources to develop an historical hypothesis, first in his mind, then on paper for a journal article. A music major treated music itself as a language and demonstrated how one of her own ideas for a musical composition had been translated, into black notes—"words"—on a page, then into actual language: music. In the process of conducting this research, the students observed many of the conventions of form and style in their disciplines and, equally important, came to understand why those conventions existed. They reported that they were able to write more comfortably in their subject matter areas as a result of their research.

It seems to us that the English class is the *second* best place for that kind of learning to occur. How much better it would be if subject teachers—the people who know the disciplines and who are, in many cases, doing original research—were to take responsibility for helping the students understand the processes of intellectual inquiry *and* writing. We do not think it would add greatly to the subject teacher's burden to include some discussion of language and writing at key moments in the course. The teacher might explain the specialized vocabulary of the discipline—how it developed and why it is used. She might present a survey of the various kinds of writing used—from notes to formal papers—explaining the function of each one. He might describe his own original research (or research done in college), explaining how writing played a role in getting ideas shaped and made permanent.

In this way, the subject matter teacher would, of course, teach writing, but from within his or her own area of competence. The subject teacher would not take over the English teacher's responsibilities and would not become enmeshed in the intricacies of grammar and rhetoric. Instead, he or she would simply explain how language functions in the discipline.

The students, coming to understand writing-as-process in the disciplines, would also learn that writing and research are personal, human experiences, rather than something done by automatons. We believe that their writing as well as their understanding of the subject area would be the richer for that.

MAKING INTERDISCIPLINARY WRITING ASSIGNMENTS

The traits of a good interdisciplinary assignment are those of *any* good writing assignment, and the comments and suggestions we offered in Chapters 2 and 3 are applicable here. At the same time, four additional principles are useful when one develops activities designed both to teach writing and to examine, assess, or evaluate a student's mastery of subject matter.

1. *Interdisciplinary assignments ought to include ample resources for students to discover what they need to know.* That principle may, at first glance, seem self evident, but a great many of the interdisciplinary assignments we have witnessed either leave students on their own to find materials or force them to rely exclusively on the basic textbook. In most school settings, of course, resources will be books, so we're suggesting, in effect, that the teacher make ample reading resources available through book lists and bibliographies, in-class libraries, or reserved shelves at the library. Too, the instructor should spend time describing these and other appropriate resources like interviews, films and tapes, magazine and journal articles.

2. *The assignment ought to encourage, or at least allow for, a variety of modes of discourse.* English teachers have a tendency to become "monogeneric," assigning only one kind of writing, frequently the five paragraph essay of literary explication. Subject teachers can similarly become locked into one limited form, say, the lab report or the technical report or the précis. The full range of discourse forms ought to be open to new writers, for students can write comfortably and creatively in forms ranging from the essay to poetry. While not every assignment need offer such options, we think that at regular intervals subject teachers ought to send their students into new territory: "This time, write it as a short story . . . or play . . . or film script."

3. *The assignment should allow the student to discover the processes of the discipline and the forms of writing in the discipline.* In English assignments, we oppose prescribing a form of discourse in advance and asking students to match its structures. Like a good English assignment, content area writing ought to allow students to learn the conventions of writing through actual experience, through the process of grappling with ideas and getting them down on paper. Of course, some conventions are idiosyncratic and need to be taught. (Many psychology journals, for example, use a footnote form that capitalizes only the first word of titles.) But the basic structures of language must emerge as the student finds and orders his or her ideas for a readership. In addition, a good interdisciplinary writing assignment will also allow the students to understand the processes of the discipline more thoroughly, engaging them in the activity of learning in the discipline, not just writing about it.

4. *The assignment should promote new learning and discovery.* By that we do not mean to suggest that students who are novices in a discipline will need to make earth-shattering new findings every time they write. But we think students should discover new things—for themselves—through writing. The writing experience should not call merely for recitation of facts and

concepts, but for synthesis and application. What students learn through writing should be new for them.

It should be noted that these four principles do not call for the subject teacher to become an English teacher; nor, for that matter, do they require that the English teacher become a subject matter specialist. Both English and subject teachers can make assignments successfully, working from their particular strengths and background knowledge. The key to success rests with principle #4, writing as discovery, for if subject matter assignments genuinely possess this quality, the rest—the finding of resources, organizing and structuring writing, even the selection of an appropriate form of discourse—will happen naturally.

The four assignments that follow illustrate these principles.

FOUR INTERDISCIPLINARY ASSIGNMENTS

SCIENCE DIALOGUES.   John Wilkes (1978), Lecturer in Science Writing at the University of Southern California, Santa Cruz, has his students create fictional dialogues to explore their understanding of science concepts. He suggests that the dialogues be kept short (600 words, 3−4 minutes) and has them written for popular, nonspecialist audiences. The students create two roles, an *announcer* or interlocutor and a *science editor* or science specialist. The topics for the dialogues may range from reports of new discoveries to discussions of the political implications of those discoveries. Two of his students' dialogues, one on the possibilities for constructing cities in outer space, the other on harvesting of dolphins by tuna fishermen, have been picked up by CBS radio for actual production.

There are a number of advantages to this assignment over the conventional report. In taking on two roles, students are forced to think about each issue from several points of view. In writing for a nonspecialist audience, they must translate their science knowledge into comprehensible terms, and when they write from the point of view of a science expert, students must understand the procedures of the discipline, not just facts and concepts. Of course, when he has his students submit their scripts to a commercial radio station, Wilkes also builds in a real audience, elevating the assignment from simply an exercise.

LANDSCAPE HISTORY.   Professor John Stilgoe (1977) of the Department of Visual and Environmental Studies and the Department of Landscape Architecture at Harvard moves his students outside the classroom to study the evolution of the architectural environment in which they live. Among the topics his students investigate are:

The reuse of railroad stations, schools, gas stations.

The use of skylights.

The history of prefabricated buildings.

Private swimming pools.

Farm artifacts in the suburbs.

Stilgoe writes:

> *Sometimes students investigate topics of personal meaning—company towns, three-deckers, urban parks, military posts—but more often they choose landscape elements related to other courses. Economics students will analyze shopping streets, psychology majors will study suburban privacy, and literature concentrators will compare the settings of novels against reconstructed landscapes. Beyond serving as a powerful adjunct to other disciplines, landscape history sharpens students' visual and verbal capacity. (p. 10)*

We applaud the way Stilgoe makes the connection between perceiving and describing, as well as his view of the role language plays in connecting all disciplines. The nature of the original research makes this an exciting, intrinsically motivating assignment, though were we using it in our own classes, we would be inclined to offer alternatives to the conventional term paper. Students might do audiovisual presentations using slides of their landscape phenomenon or prepare their reports in the form of an illustrated magazine.

ART AND WRITING. Susan Breakey (1980), an art teacher from Chesaning, Michigan, suggests having students explore the origins of the alphabet as an interdisciplinary project. Her students examine Chinese characters, Egyptian hieroglyphics, Babylonian wall reliefs, and American Indian pictographs. The students then create a symbolic language of their own, exploring ways and means of representing experience on paper. This assignment strikes us as especially useful for English teachers because it opens up important areas of discussion about the nature of language and symbolic systems. One can see an entire unit on general semantics and communications problems blossoming from this activity.

Breakey's project is similar to one conducted by Richard Reid (1977) at Newton North High School in Massachusetts. He works with Japanese ideographs showing the evolution of present-day characters from earlier, drawn forms. In the process, he engages students in discussion of Japanese culture and how it influenced the development of abstract, stylized characters from literal pictures.

TECHNICAL WRITING. Earlier in the chapter we wrote critically of some technical writing assignments that place emphasis on form to the exclusion of process and content. In contrast, we will present the work of one of our colleagues at Central Michigan University, William Lewis (1978), who gives what impress us as two very well-constructed technical writing assignments.

The first of these is the "Product Research Report." Students choose a common product that is made by several competing manufacturers: nail polish, lipstick, ball-point pens, batteries. Then, in the fashion of *Consumer Reports*, they design a series of tests to determine which brands are superior. The students do detailed analyses of the products (learning a good deal of scientific methodology along the way) and then prepare a succinct report (mastering the forms of technical writing in the process).

The second assignment is the "Survey Report," in which students choose a contemporary issue—diets, drugs, economics—and create a questionnaire based on Gallup or Harris-type polls. The students generate key questions (thus discussing the issues themselves), create and test an opinionnaire, and finally interview people and report the results. Like the product evaluation, this activity also engages students in discovering information while learning how to write about it successfully.

Further, both assignments have built-in audience appeal. Because the students work in small groups that investigate a number of different products and issues, Lewis reports that interest in the final presentations is extremely high.

PLANNING THE INTERDISCIPLINARY UNIT

Thus far we have concentrated our attention principally on individual interdisciplinary assignments—writing that might come as a part of class exploration of a topic, possibly serving as an examination or culminating activity. However, for interdisciplinary writing to become a matter of habit for students, it is useful for them to see it as being more than one shot, something done at the end of the unit. We are excited by the possibilities for constructing interdisciplinary *units*, blocks of instruction that can extend over a period of time—several weeks, a month, an entire term or course. A good interdisciplinary unit involves writing, not just at the end, but as an integral part of the learning process. Such units can be designed for use in English or subject area classes, though the best of all possible arrangements is for them to be conducted by several faculty members, each coaching from his or her own area of expertise.

CHOOSING A TOPIC. Considerable care has to be taken in choosing a topic for interdisciplinary study, if only because the students may be spending a long period of time with it—it will need to have some substance and staying power. At the same time, virtually any topic one can dream up can be developed successfully. James Beck (1980) of the University of Wisconsin at Whitewater remarks:

> *Appropriate topics for interdisciplinary interpretation are, quite literally, great and small. Topics can include objects and processes (a horse; a river in Michigan); they can include events and recurring concerns (the fall of Rome, why Americans value work and the future); they can include minor concerns (why do people wear sunglasses?) and major (why people migrate); they can include issues: the currently controversial (alcohol use, pollution, crime), the standard (sports, bureaucracy, the automobile), and the timeless and the philosophical (human nature, community and alienation, self and society). (pp. 28–29)*

Naturally, the teacher teaching independently would want to pick a topic fairly close to his or her area of expertise. The science teacher would probably be most interested in topics like Ecology, Medicine, or Weather; the history/social studies teacher might want to examine subjects like Australia, American Indians, the United Nations, or Rome; the English teacher might be oriented to literary themes like Coming of Age, Voyages, Utopia, or Family. But virtually any topic—Farming, Lions, Locomotives, Oceans, Circuses, Time, to name just a few—can be developed from the points of view of several disciplines in both the sciences and the humanities.

IDENTIFY THE ISSUES AND PROBLEMS. Obviously such topics, as stated, are much too broad to deal with successfully. At the same time, we find unrealistic the traditional concept of "narrowing the topic" which would have the writer whittle "Oceans" down to "Ponds in My Neighborhood" or "Time" into "The Restoration of the Town Hall Clock."

A more productive approach is to have students identify a variety of issues, problems, and concerns, then select from those the ones that seem to merit in-depth investigation. Careful guidance of the teacher is required at this stage, and we proceed in two steps, using discussion and brainstorming techniques.

First, we ask, "What do we already know about this topic?" It's safe to assume that with almost any issue, students already have some background knowledge, and it is important that their information and ideas are not ignored. Sometimes we will do this as a listmaking activity, with students using freewriting or free association to get down their thoughts. The purpose at this point is to establish a community storehouse of knowledge from which the class can operate.

Second, we continue, "What do we want to know or discover?" That, in itself, is too broad a question, so we refine it. "What seem to be the central issues? What are the key problems? What simply makes you curious?" The answers are listed on the board—a laundry list, with no ideas or questions rejected as being inappropriate or irrelevant.

Sometimes it is helpful to prime the class for this discussion by using written materials: short fiction or nonfiction or possibly even a poem. Thus a class taking up the Ecology theme might read or listen to Sarah Orne Jewett's "The White Heron" which deals with a young girl's struggle over whether to reveal the location of a heron's nest to an older boy she idolizes. Or the teacher might read a point/counterpoint article on the needs of technology and fiscal growth versus the protection of the environment.

Eventually, the diverse questions on the board are narrowed, combined, and rewritten to create a smaller number of key questions, the basic issues. Depending on the topic, these might be as few as four or five or as many as twenty or thirty. The group writing "assignment" at this point is to create tight, articulate questions that genuinely reflect its interest.

DISCUSS THE CONTRIBUTIONS OF THE DISCIPLINES. James Beck, cited earlier, uses the term "representative realism" to discuss an interdisciplinary point of view. He suggests that each discipline takes both a specialized and a narrow point of view in examining problems. The specialization leads to important insights, but it also narrows the line of vision. Thus the microbiologist may visualize the universe in terms of billions and billions of tiny organisms and offer important insights into the human condition (as does Lewis Thomas in *The Lives of a Cell*). But in focusing on the small unit, he may also lose focus of some of the broad, sweeping forces at work on humankind that a futurist might find interesting (Alvin Toffler, *The Third Wave*).

Beck argues, and we agree, that students should recognize these disciplinary blinders and learn to assess the contribution that each discipline can make to solving problems and answering questions. For his college classes Beck prepares a checklist of disciplines: *theology, fine arts, literature, history, biography, psychology, sociology, anthropology, ethnology, political sciences, technology, linguistics, biology, chemistry, physics,* and so on. For each discipline the students then ask, "What can it tell me about my problem?" Of course, not every discipline will shed light on all topics, but we find in our teaching that a surprising number of connections can be made.

LOCATING RESOURCES. Throughout this chapter we have stressed the importance of making resources for interdisciplinary writing readily available. For many units, an in-class library of titles might be sufficient for students to find the necessary materials to answer their questions. But more often the search will go beyond the classroom and extend outside print literature. We supply our students with yet another checklist suggesting resources:

The arts: photography, painting, sculpture, dance, mime, opera, symphony, jazz, rock, architecture, ceramics.

Community resources

Businesses, which can supply speakers, interviewees, tours, pamphlets, films.

Colleges and universities, rich in human resources and materials.

City, county, state, and Federal agencies, offering books, films, pamphlets, slide shows.

Clubs and organizations, including service groups, special interest or hobby clubs, historical societies, arts workshops.

People, amateurs and professionals, hobbyists and raconteurs.

The library, which includes much more than books and can supply films, slides, book talks, speakers, and reference services.

Popular culture, including television, film, best sellers, magazines, radio, advertising.

Museums: art, history, natural history.

"Happenings": recitals, concerts, plays, parades, lectures, discussions, strikes, protests.

WRITING, REWRITING, PUBLISHING.   As students proceed through the unit their work becomes more and more individualized. They choose a question that they want to answer and explore the available resources. They take notes, talk over ideas, and eventually began to consider solutions to their problems and about ways of presenting their findings to the group. The mode of presentation need not be limited to the formal report or the term paper. Students may write fiction or nonfiction; they may decide to make a media presentation in film or videotape; they may write a script for a play; they may work as individuals, in small groups, or occasionally as a whole class.

A SAMPLE UNIT: THE ME TREE.   Almost any interdisciplinary unit becomes complex when students conduct research into a variety of questions and pursuing individual projects. A complete unit is thus too long to present here. We would like to offer a sample of the possibilities, and since many of our illustrations have been chosen from college courses, we'll select an example from elementary school, third grade. "The Me Tree" was developed by some of our students in a course in writing for elementary teachers at Central Michigan University (Bauer, et al., 1979). The students followed a planning method outlined by Shirley Heck (1979) in which the various disciplines are represented as the limbs of a tree. (See the figure on page 88) The "Me" in the title refers to the individual third grader: the unit was one on self-understanding.

Among the projects proposed by the authors were:

Language arts

Describe yourself to someone who has never met you. Let that person come to know "the real you" through words.

Keep a personal journal of your thoughts and feelings, exploring your day-to-day life and the things that happen to you.

Social Studies

Write a short history of the origin of your name, first or last.

Create a family tree, tracing your roots as far back as you can.

Teach others in the class some games you like to play with members of your family.

Mathematics and Science

Study good eating habits. Then bring in empty food containers and set up a store. Write out good and bad shopping lists for a family of four.

Read up on the digestive system. Draw a chart and write captions and notations to show what happens to your food when it is digested.

Put together a time capsule including information about you and your friends such as snapshots, journal notes, tape recordings, poems. Arrange to have it opened in the school twenty-five years from now.

Pretend you have been reduced in size and are traveling in a friend's body. Describe what you see.

Music

Write a series of poems describing your feelings at various times. Then find music to accompany or illustrate it.

Write down what happens in your head when you listen to favorite pieces of music. What do you hear? What do you see?

Art

Lie down on a big sheet of butcher paper and have somebody trace around you. Then draw in the internal organs and label them.

Take your best writing from this unit and prepare a book of it. Illustrate the stories, essays, or poems. Prepare and decorate a cover.

Me Tree

Physical Education

Look in the mirror. Write a description of yourself as you are. If there are any parts you'd like to change, describe this ideal you.

Invent a "road test" for your body. If you were about to buy a car, you'd like to drive it first. If you were going to pick a new body, you'd want to test it out. Write down your test, then test some bodies and report on the results.

Write a short story about an athlete who "freaks out" under the pressure at a game.

Invent a sport and write the rules.

Once again, those suggestions are just a sampler of possibilities. The authors of "The Me Tree" were able to come up with hundreds of writing activities, and they developed a bibliography of several hundred titles, probably more than any teacher would ever want to use. But the thoroughness of their work helps one see the unlimited potential of what we are calling "interdisciplinary writing."

CHAPTER 5

REVISING, EDITING, CORRECTING

In the conventional model of composition teaching, the teacher is the final arbiter of "good writing." The teacher sets the criteria for what is interesting, logical, effective, or moving. The teacher is also responsible for noting and informing students of linguistic *faux pas* and stylistic infelicities, as well as pointing out errors in usage in mechanics. And, in the conventional model, the composing process is given short shrift. The student writes the paper and hands it in to the teacher, who reads it, marks it, grades it and hands it back to the student, who glances at the end of the paper to see the grade and tucks it away in a notebook (or drops it in a wastebasket on the way out of the room).

Current practices in teaching composition offer significant alternatives to the conventional model. Most important, perhaps, is that focusing on writing as process encourages teachers to teach drafting and revising, helping students to learn to define and refine their ideas while they are writing. Thus many matters generally taken up at the teacher-as-theme-grader stage are now handled in process, *while* students are writing rather than *after* they have finished. Teachers are recognizing the importance of integrating concern for correctness, usage, and mechanics at the appropriate stages of the writing process, instead of placing heavy emphasis on correctness throughout the entire writing assignment.

We think most writing instructors have come to accept the principle that evaluation of writing is best done in process. Yet, in practice, many have difficulty establishing the activities that teach students the necessary editing skills. We know many teachers who have tried to organize their classes into small group editorial circles—a major technique in our approach to revision—and have abandoned the idea, saying that "It just didn't work." The students either did not feel comfortable in the groups or did not work on the task at hand. Some small groups got out of control and became hostile and negative, while others gave hollow, meaningless advice.

It's not surprising that students (and their instructors) experience problems when they initiate a writing workshop. Many of the students may have had very little experience with writing, having been trained in classes that favored workbooks over actual composition. Thus they are working in a medium that is foreign to them, making them uncomfortable. They have difficulty in clarifying what they think, let along drafting a paper. If getting an idea down in the first place is difficult, asking students to make ideas and expression better through second and third drafts is a mind-boggling task.

Further, even the students who do have some writing experience may have gained it in classrooms when the teacher has been the one with all the answers. The students have merely been told what to write and handed their papers in to the teacher to get comments on the goodness or badness of what they have done. Often teacher reactions have been little more than proof-reading symbols indicating problems with usage, spelling, and mechanics, and students have had few thoughtful responses to the content of their work.

It is little wonder that students come into a revision workshop with considerable resistance. Not only do they feel uninformed about how to write, but they know little about rewriting as well. Many of our students think that good writing is writing that is error free; thus they see revision as nothing more than elimination of mistakes. When we ask our students at the beginning of the term about the problems they have had with their writing, "grammar" surfaces most often as a primary concern.

It is precisely these problems that point toward the need for more work on revision with students, especially in a writing workshop where students take responsibility for editing one another's pieces. It is a legitimate goal of any writing program to help students become independent writers—people who can write and revise on their own. Since they are ill equipped to revise when they come into our classes, we feel it is our obligation to teach them.

How can one go about setting up a writing workshop that will be successful? How can one teach the revision process? How can students be helped to become their own editors? How can they be helped to improve their papers through revision? How can copyreading be made a part of the revision process that they will use? These are the fundamental questions we want to examine in the following sections.

THE WORKSHOP APPROACH TO REVISION

We begin by describing the nature of the revising/correcting process to our students. We make a key distinction between *revising*, which involves moving around words and sentences and adjusting content, and *correcting* or *copyreading*, which centers on usage and mechanics. We explain that correctness is a means to an end—successfully reaching an audience—but that it is not necessarily an end in itself. Further, we stress that revising is much more complex and time consuming than is correcting. We describe how real writers prepare many, many drafts, revising their work again and again until it says precisely what they want it to say.

Then we explain the purpose of the writing workshop as a way of helping students work on writing in progress, solving problems as they emerge rather than waiting for somebody else to tell them what they've done wrong. We discuss the importance of thinking about the audience for one's writing, and we explain that the workshop can serve as an audience of real readers whose reactions will give writers insight into what is effective in their writing and what can be strengthened through revision. We suggest that even novice writers can learn to draw on one another's strengths and perceptions in working on writing drafts and revisions.

Often students have doubts about the potential of the writing workshop and are skeptical that they can learn to edit their own writing successfully. They have come to see the teacher as the writing guru, and it takes some time and effort for them to become independent learners. Consequently, at the outset of the revision workshop, the teacher needs to provide a means for helping students take gradual steps toward independence.

WRITERS AS EDITORS

In *The Reader Over Your Shoulder*, Robert Graves and Richard Hodge (1943) give advice for writers:

> *We suggest that whenever anyone sits down to write, he should imagine a crowd of his prospective readers (rather than a grammarian in cap and gown) looking over his shoulder. They will be asking such questions as: "What does this sentence mean?" "Why do you trouble to tell me that again?" "Why have you chosen such a ridiculous metaphor?" "Must I really read this long, limping sentence?" "Haven't you got your ideas muddled here?" By anticipating and listing as many questions of this sort as possible, the writer will discover certain tests of intelligibility to which he may regularly submit his work . . . . (p. 19)*

Writers need to become conscious of how others will react. They need to develop a reasonably objective stance toward what they have written so they can look at it as if someone else had written it. Of course, that skill is difficult to develop. For a student struggling to finish a paper, anything that is down and on the page looks pretty good. (That is not just a problem for students; most adult writers have it too.) We find we can help students through the use of questions such as the following, taken from Lou Kelly's *From Dialogue to Discourse* (1972):

To anticipate a reader's reaction to your writing style, read aloud what you write.

Do you hear and feel some movement, some rhythm as you read? If not, what keeps your sentences from sounding easy and natural?

Are they stiff and awkward because you've put words together in combinations that are difficult to read, combinations you would not use when talking? . . .

To answer all those questions, you will, most likely, need some help—from a competent and sympathetic editor. . . . So . . . You need to learn to recognize and eliminate the kinds of "debris" that slow down the movement of your sentences—and your ideas. (p. 246)

At first students may feel unconfident about their impressions of their own writing and will have difficulty answering questions like these. But if the process is continued—with other discussions and critiques during the writing workshop—the students will become clearer, more precise, and more detailed in their answers. We change questions from one session to another, encouraging students to look at a wide range of features in their writing, everything from word choice to content.

Another approach to help students develop consciousness of what they are doing in writing is to have them to write or talk about their drafts, why they chose to write on the particular topic they did. In answering that question, they talk about the importance of the subject in their own lives, and they describe the kind of reaction they thought they might get from their audience. "A lot of people are interested in the Olympics just now, so I thought they might be interested in them" "My brother works at a nuclear power plant, so I had lots of information available." "I felt I could explain this clearly, because I've known a lot of people who've been through this kind of experience." As students talk about the topic and their approach to it, they often discover that they know even more about it or that they can refocus their paper to broaden the audience appeal.

A related question extends students' thinking on the choice of topics. "What other topics did you consider and why did you reject them?" Students may discuss their choices in class with their peers, or they may prefer to write about the topics they rejected and to read their statements silently. Frequently, one student in the class may have picked a topic rejected by someone else, and that can lead to an interesting discussion of the selection of material and alternative approaches to it.

Students can also learn to reconsider how they have written their papers through careful assessment of the audience. Often we ask our students to answer another set of questions after they have completed a rough draft:

Describe the audience for which this paper is intended.

How old a group is it?

Who are its members?

What do they have in common?

What are their values, interests, and concerns?

How do you think your audience will be affected by your paper?

Why?

Students may have gone astray in their writing, losing sight of the audience or changing audiences or purposes in the middle, and these questions help them focus on their original plan once again. Sometimes the students will realize that their plan needs to be changed. Occasionally, they may decide that they were writing for the wrong audience, or that their material is wrong for the audience they are trying to reach. In any case, the questions lead the way to directed, purposeful revision.

Revision is especially difficult for many students in opinion and argumentative papers. Many inexperienced writers tend to argue what they have heard or been taught all their lives, or they present generally accepted, stereotypic opinions without really thinking them through. The argument papers seem overgeneralized and undersupported. Further, students seem blind to these flaws, and, because their opinions are at stake, they are resentful toward the suggestion that their arguments are weak or simplistic.

To help students learn to revise these kinds of papers and, as Graves and Hodge suggest, to learn to anticipate audience response, we use a teaching technique common to debate: having students argue the other side of the case. When they come to class with a draft of a paper describing a strong opinion, we have them write a response to their own work, using the strongest opposing points of view that they can imagine. "Counter every argument you made in your original paper," we tell them. "Use the best counterarguments you can think of. Use any additional arguments that you have heard that are in opposition to your own." It is difficult for students to take on the values of someone who is quite unlike them and to offer that viewpoint with any conviction. But we push our students, prodding and even provoking, not letting them set up any straw men or women. Most important, the process clearly helps students recognize that one has to anticipate the best arguments of the opposition in order to be convincing in setting forth one's own.

Another activity that helps students learn to become their own editors is to have them do some freewriting *after* the rough draft has been completed. We ask the students to do additional, stream-of-consciousness writing on the topic. They may write about material they were not able to include, review counterarguments (as described above), discuss the writing process as they experienced it, or amplify their main points. The technique draws on Peter Elbow's claim in *Writing without Teachers* (1974) that one cannot edit writing "till you have something to edit":

> *If you have written a lot, if you have digressed and wandered into some interesting areas and accumulated some interesting material (more than you can see any unity in), and if, at last, a center of gravity has emerged and you find yourself finally saying to yourself, "Yes, I now see what I'm driving at, now I see what I've been stumbling around trying to say," you are finally in a position to start mopping up—to start editing.* (p. 38)

Elbow places a great deal of emphasis on mopping up after loosely written first drafts have been prepared, and our "postwriting freewriting" is useful because it helps the writer gain a sense of perspective on what he or she has prepared. It may be that the "center of gravity" for the piece will emerge, not in the first draft, but in the freewriting. Certainly many of our students discover things left out through this process and go on to write richer, more substantial drafts.

But this technique is also useful with another kind of student, the very careful writer, who is concerned about making mistakes or turning in a perfect first draft. Such a writer may actually begin to edit too soon for fear of letting the paper get out of hand. This student will often cut out ideas before they have been explored, and his or her writing will lack complexity of thought or richness of detail. "What else do you have to say about this?" we ask them when they have finished a draft. "Now that the formal writing is over, free associate about the paper." Often we find the informal writing will be more vigorous than the first draft and, seeing that, students can embark on a successful revision.

PEERS AS EDITORS

We began this discussion by examining ways of helping students become their own editors, for in the end, the independent writer must be able to rely on his or her own skills for writing in the real world. At the same time, using peers as editors greatly nourishes the in-class editorial process. Often peers have a kind of detachment from another person's paper that allows them to make extremely helpful editorial suggestions. In addition, we are firmly persuaded that there is "transfer" from learning how to help another person with a paper and the long-range goal of helping students learn to revise their own work. But learning these editorial skills is not automatic.

Simply pairing up students and letting them have a go at editing is seldom successful; in fact, it can be utterly destructive in the writing class. We introduce peer editing in two stages: first, *responding;* second, *evaluating and editing.*

Responding is one of the most difficult skills to teach. It does not involve a formal evaluation or a critique of a paper, something students have come to expect in a writing class. Instead, it calls for the reader to describe impressions—what the paper did for him or her. It is our assumption that even before writers receive evaluative comments and suggestions for change that they need to know how their piece affected the reader. Adults need this kind of response, too, and more than once we've found ourselves saying to a critic, "Yes, yes, I know the middle is too long and stuffy, but tell me, *what did you think?*"

"What did you think?" That's what the reader wants to hear. "What went on in your mind when you read this?" "Do you agree?" "Did I move you— even just a little?" Response may not always be positive, and it may not give the writer the feeling he or she has been completely successful—but it is a *reaction.*

Response needs to be focused in order to be helpful. (A common response that lacks focus is "Oh, wow." It provides a global response, but nothing that is of specific help to the writer.) We use three strategies to help students focus their responses.

READING ALOUD. We don't recommend oral reading for the very youngest students, who tend to be text-bound, word-for-word readers, but the technique can be very useful for older writers. One of the first problems we face when we ask students to respond to a paper is that the readers often give the paper a cursory examination and a facile response. Therefore, when students come to class with rough drafts to share, we ask them to begin by having the writer read the paper aloud. This way, nobody misses anything, and often the oral reading itself is enough to generate a response. Frequently, listeners will jump in with comments, and the reader/writer can get a sense of where the paper had impact on the audience. At the end, because all the listeners have heard every word of the paper, the discussion tends to flow well. After the students have heard every word of the paper one time, they may reread it silently and jot down their responses and reactions.

THE RUNNING COMMENTARY. Another technique we use early in the term to push students toward more careful reading and focused response is the running commentary. Again students share rough drafts, and rather than just asking them to read and respond to their partners' papers, we have them place check marks in the margin where words, phrases, or sentences made an impact on them, then go back and jot down their responses. Through the running commentary they become quite specific, even though they may not respond to every feature in the paper.

LETTERS TO THE AUTHOR.   In some classes, students are extremely reluctant to share their papers publicly. They balk at reading their own writing aloud and are reluctant even to share papers for silent reading. To overcome this problem—an understandable one given the public humiliation often attached to writing errors—we use the letter to the author. Papers are exchanged, but anonymously. (Students may place a code number at the top of their paper or use a pen name.) The reader/responder then writes a letter back to the author describing reactions. We find that the letter format also helps to move students away from formal criticism—after all, most letters are friendly, not hostile. The writer is then able to digest the responses of the letter writer. Once letters have been exchanged and it appears that the responses are reasonably positive, the students are very curious and want to abandon anonymity. "Who wrote this letter?" "Who was the author of the dog story?" "Who was Superwriter?"

The line between responding and evaluating is a very fine one, for evaluation and subsequent editorial advice flow naturally from a response. But evaluation, in contrast to response, focuses on the revision process—the "what next" or the "how can I improve it?" We emphasize to our students that evaluation should be helpful, not hurtful, and that it should be directed toward the paper itself, not at the traits of the person who wrote it. While professional critics may become vindictive toward an author, we see no justification for allowing students to confuse personal behavior with writing skills.

Often we use the response techniques, *reading aloud, running commentary,* and *letter to the author* as the starting point for evaluation and editing, but we employ the following strategies and techniques as well.

ORAL AND WRITTEN CRITIQUES.   We distribute copies of papers either to the entire class (which isn't always possible because of copying costs) or to small groups (more reasonable, particularly if students are asked to make several carbons of their drafts). All members of a class or group are given an opportunity to comment orally on papers, and in addition, several people are assigned to do formal written critiques as a follow-up.

Early in the term we join the oral discussion as a way of providing models of ways to react. We talk about what we liked or enjoyed in the paper, pointing out its successful elements; then we make limited numbers of suggestions about how the paper might be improved. Soon students join in the discussion by sharing their reactions, whether those reactions involve confusion over the meaning of a paper, arguments counter to those presented, additional evidence that might be used, similar experience with different outcomes, or questions and suggestions about more effective ways of structuring or developing content.

Both the oral and written reactions to papers become lengthier and cover a wider variety of issues as students become more competent readers, more certain of their own sense of the qualities of good writing, more able to describe those qualities to someone else. We also invite divergent reactions, allowing people to use both personal experience and the text of the paper as support for their arguments.

As students share their critiques of papers, they learn not only about techniques for making their writing stronger and more interesting, but they gain a sense of the elements of good writing as well. It is not uncommon for students to raise points about the main focus, mood, or tone of a piece of writing; to distinguish between motivated and unmotivated action; to demand concrete details and telling evidence; to question the elements of logic. Of course, they do not use the terminology of rhetoric here, but it is important to observe that even in unguided discussions these concerns come up. In short, the peer evaluation of writing is anything but unsophisticated and imprecise.

THE DEVIL'S ADVOCATE.   We have already mentioned the technique of having writers anticipate the arguments that will be raised against their papers. As part of peer group criticism, it is useful to have the students write a devil's advocate paper, in which one student responds to another's paper by raising all the counterarguments he or she can come up with.

ANALYSIS OF THE AUTHOR.   Just as writers need to be concerned about reaching their intended audiences, they need also to be concerned about how the audience perceives them. In this activity we have students bring rough drafts of papers to class without actual names on them (again codes or pen names are used). We then collect the papers and redistribute them. We tell the responders to the papers to write a character sketch of the author based on what they know about him/her from reading the paper. What does the author look like? Is the author a male or a female? What gives you that impression? What are the author's important values? Is the author aggressive, timid, confident, shy, strong, weak, funny, serious? The students should describe the author's personality, values, beliefs, and disposition on the basis of the paper and explain why they have described the author this way. Naturally, we do not allow these comments to become personal or insulting. The paper readers are attempting to describe the writer's *persona*, his or her image on paper, not writing a character sketch of the person based only on analysis of writing style and content.

In this activity, both the responder and the author learn something about how language communicates messages about the writer. Furthermore, the author learns where he or she is taking too much for granted or is distorting or exaggerating what he or she believes. Such insights provide information useful in revising.

PEER EDITING: SOME LOGISTICAL CONSIDERATIONS

We think it's a good idea to set up various kinds of classroom configurations for editing student papers, giving students a variety of audiences and a range of comments. Sometimes in-depth analysis is particularly important to a writer, and this can best be done by an editing partner; at other times, numerous short reactions may be more helpful, and for this, commentary by the whole class is appropriate.

PAIRS. We usually begin a peer editing program in a writing class by having the students work in pairs. We find that a one-to-one relationship is less threatening to writers than a larger group. Pairs of writers also tend to develop an informal support system that may last throughout a course, so that even when the class is working in larger groups, people who were buddies at the beginning of the course will spontaneously seek each other out for advice and suggestions.

The instructor may want to assign the pairs or to let people choose their own partners. Whenever possible, we prefer to have the selection be voluntary. However, if teachers have insights into personalities and the writing strengths and weaknesses of individuals, they might want to structure or assign pairs for optimal strength.

The advantage of having students work in pairs is, obviously, that they have the time to work in great depth on one another's papers (and, practically, that extra copies of papers are not required). If it is early in the course, you may want to establish activities, guides, and questions of the sort developed by Lou Kelly (described earlier). Later in the term you may simply be able to say, "Work together in pairs on your papers," and no further guidance will be necessary.

The instructor should also provide help as needed to prod the pairs into successful action. In the field of creative dramatics there is a process called "side coaching," where, working on the sidelines, teachers intervene as necessary to help an improvised drama along. They may call out a suggestion, "How do you feel about that? Show it in your expression." Or they may manipulate the drama by changing the plot: "There is a phone call. It is your mother telling you your brother has been killed in an automobile accident."

Occasionally the side coach may even take up a role in the drama, walking on stage and taking a part in the play.

All three forms of side coaching seem appropriate for peer editing. Sometimes the writing coach may just walk past the writers and, sensing that something is needed, offer direct suggestions: "I think you've spent enough time on that opening paragraph. Why don't you have a look at the next couple of pages?" He or she may want to coach readers in ways of responding: "Tom, tell Denise how you feel about that character. I mean, really tell her." Sometimes, the coach may join a pair, making it a threesome, and participate directly by giving direct responses. No one teacher role should dominate—especially direct participation—but it should also be very clear to the students that they have not been utterly abandoned in their pairs.

SMALL GROUPS. Having students work in groups of four to six is the mainstay of our peer editing program. The groups are large enough so that a student can get several responses to a paper—preferably responses that diverge somewhat in their opinions—yet small enough so that they can develop a sense of community and interdependence.

Small group work also requires somewhat more advanced organizing than having students work in pairs. The students will need to know in advance when small group workshop days will take place and when they are to bring their rough drafts to class. Ideally, students can bring as many copies of their paper to class as there are members of their discussion group. That way, each member can not only hear the writing but see it. Copies can be carbons (uncorrected to save time and energy, we tell our students), dittoed, mimeographed, or even photocopied. Copying is relatively inexpensive, but even so, some instructors (and possibly their budget-conscious administrators) feel that requiring copies is too expensive. In that case, students can pass papers around the group so that everyone has a chance to read and possibly to make notes about one another's papers before beginning a discussion.

Like the makeup of pairs, the constitution of small groups is of concern to the instructor. You may wish to begin by assigning a group of students to work together. Perhaps you have read some of their writing and you have determined which students seem to be stronger and more highly motivated and which have difficulty with writing. Balancing groups of writers helps to assure that the groups will get something from the experience and that there won't be groups totally lacking in experience and motivation.

We also like to vary groups so that sometimes students are placed in particular groups, while at other times they are free to choose with whom they want to work. However, in self-selected groups we have found that serious writers often tend to select others of their kind to work with, while the less able and less motivated wind up together. Sometimes, we take what are basically self-selected groups and make one or two changes to insure diversity.

Some instructors are concerned that in mixed ability groups the better writers won't get any help with their writing, and that they will, in fact, be dissuaded from attending to editing tasks by the less motivated writers. Occasionally, in our experience, that concern has been warranted. We remedy that problem in several ways.

First, as with pairs, we provide structure for small group discussions early in the term. We supply discussion checklists and encourage the students to focus on a particular detail or quality in writing. Every student in the group needs to complete the guide questions for each paper, so the attention of the group is kept on writing.

Second, we continue to side coach, remaining active ourselves in the workshop. We circulate from group to group, listen to readings of papers, monitor group discussions, add our own questions, work to bring out quiet members of the group, ask students to read what they have written on their editing sheets or reaction papers, clarify the task, and, in general, help groups understand and complete the assignment successfully.

Though it occasionally happens that more sophisticated writers do not get the kind of help they need, at the same time it seems to us an excellent learning experience for the good writers to help out the less good. Their leadership is required, and we find that they often become quite skillful at articulating strengths and weaknesses in others' papers. Just as tutoring someone else can be a learning experience for the tutor, good writers find that working with people of less ability does not diminish their skills, but enhances them. Further, though we think peer group editing is important, we do not dismiss the importance of teacher comments, as we will show in the next section. If something is missed in small group work, the teacher can always compensate while doing his/her own reading and response.

WHOLE CLASS DISCUSSION.   Working with class response as a whole is helpful in providing the writer with a variety of responses. Whole class reading is also as close to a real audience that one can get within the confines of a composition classroom. In leading the whole class discussion, the instructor has the opportunity to guide students' thinking to points of particular appropriateness and to model ways in which the students can respond to papers when working in pairs and small groups. As students hear other responses, they begin to sharpen their own notions about good writing.

Many students are shy and reluctant to have their papers read or presented to the whole class. Equally a problem, students lack confidence in the validity of their own responses and thus decline to make public comments. The instructor must be extremely skilled in group dynamics and must be reassuring to the students if whole class analysis is to work.

With large classes it is not practical to duplicate papers for every student. Some teachers use the opaque projector to flash a copy of the paper on a screen. We prefer to have multiple copies of perhaps two or three papers made (seldom can one discuss more than that in a class hour anyway), so that students have the piece under discussion in their hands. In the course of a term, each student might have one or two of his/her papers run off for reading by the entire class.

Though a few students do not mind identifying themselves on papers that will be discussed by the whole class, we have found that students are often freer and more honest in their reactions to papers if they don't know who the writer is. In fact, even if they do know the identify of the writer, they are more willing to talk if the writer's name doesn't appear. Thus we preserve the anonymity of our students, while regretting that past bad experiences with public readings make it necessary.

We generally follow up whole class analyses by having the students prepare short written critiques. Sometimes every person in the class will write a reaction to each paper that is discussed. More often, we assign several individuals to respond to each paper read, rotating these assignments so that every member of the class has an opportunity to write several critiques during the term. Written critiques provide considerable information that doesn't emerge when the whole class is engaged in discussion. Having more detailed critiques gives the writer concrete suggestions about how to revise as well as the benefit of a wide range of ideas and impressions from a larger audience.

THE ROLE OF THE TEACHER IN EDITING

We think we have made it clear by now that we believe it is important for students to work on writing in progress and for teachers to supply as much help as possible during, rather than after, the fact of composition. Now we would like to turn more specifically to the teacher's role in the revision/editing part of the writing process and suggest the following guidelines.

1. *The first response of the teacher to the student should be that of a person, not a grammarian or grade giver.* Talk to the student about your reaction to his or her ideas, thoughts, opinions, and experiences. Share your own beliefs and related experiences. Let the student see clearly that you care about the writing as communication, that both the ideas and the sharing of ideas is important to you.

It is the instructor's responsibility to make certain that the discussion of the paper is handled sensitively. Although we want students to be concrete in their analyses, we do not want the writer to be devastated by negative reactions to subject, style, organization, and mechanics. We remind our students that their function is to serve as editors and to isolate the elements of the paper that can be improved to make it a success.

On the other hand, some students are so sensitive to the feelings of others that they do not want to make negative comments at all. To help solve this problem, we remind our students that all remarks are to be directed to the paper, not to the individual, and that writers should not take comments about their writing as being judgments about their worth as human beings. Given those kinds of warnings and ground rules, our students have generally been able to join in whole class discussion successfully.

In contrast to pairs and small group sessions, where we want students to be independent writers and respondents, we maintain a more directive role in the whole class analysis, if only because it is necessary to stage manage a discussion among twenty, thirty, or more people. We also tend to select the topics or items for discussion, choosing areas where we think many members of the class need help. At the same time, whole class discussions are often freewheeling, and we wind up far from where we began or intended to go.

2. *Use conferences when possible instead of writing comments on papers.* There is no question that face-to-face conferencing is far more efficient than writing comments on students' papers, and it has the advantage of being done on school time, instead of over the weekend when you'd rather be doing something else. Use the class time as a means of talking with students individually. Read and listen to papers that are being worked on in small groups and make suggestions for students about ways to revise their papers. Make yourself available during the classroom hour for students to have individual conferences with you while others are working alone, in pairs, or in groups. Try to set aside times for more sustained conferences when students can talk to you in general terms about their growth in the course.

3. *Critically examine the effect of your written comments on student papers.* The research in composition does not support the belief that written comments on themes are effective in changing students' writing behaviors. Most teachers have had the discouraging experience of handing back a set of papers that required ten to twenty hours to mark only to have students look only at the grade and ignore the constructive comments. Before you spend another ten or twenty hours, carefully consider whether or not your comments are useful to the students, for, if they are, it seems likely that the students will respond to them. Doing this ourselves, we find that students are seldom responsive to suggestions for improving papers that are, in essence, finished. Our written responses tend to be rather like our first responses: an honest reaction to the student about the content and ideas of his or her paper.

4. *Don't mark papers if you don't need to.* This statement will probably strike composition teachers of widely different beliefs as being heretical. "Papers are to mark/correct/grade," the mythology goes. We are committed to the principle that students must receive *response* to what they write, but not necessarily *written response* or *critical response.* If the writing workshop includes ample provisions for audience reaction, and if the teacher has actively worked to supply editorial assistance in progress, there seems to be no reason why the teacher must spend that ten to twenty hours marking a set of papers.

5. *Make suggestions in terms of immediate student needs, not rhetorical or syntactic principles.* There seems to be a strong tendency toward excessive generalization among writing teachers. When they spy a problem in student writing, they often relate it to a general principle of composition. Thus if a paragraph is thin, the instructor provides advice in the form of suggestions on *using supporting evidence*—perhaps as covered in section 22.14 of the handbook. While these principles may be useful to the instructor in recognizing problems, they seldom provide students with direct assistance. Thus we suggest that you phrase suggestions in terms of the particular paper at hand, talking about its actual content, rather than presenting abstractions. It seems likely that if students receive adequate help with the specifics, they will come to the generalizations on their own.

6. *Make suggestions that help students solve their own problems.* By this we do not mean to play a guessing game with writers: "Can't you think of a better way to phrase this?" "Can you find the error in this sentence?" "Is that what you really meant to say?" Rather, we recognize that many problems experienced by young writers grow from lack of a sense of purpose, direction, and audience. Encourage students to talk through their aims and plans with you and, in the process, help them clarify their intentions. Often through this process of clarification the students will come to see not only their problems, but natural solutions to those problems.

7. *Encourage students to develop their own standards.* Provide support through your comments so students can develop their own definitions of good writing. Help them learn to evaluate their own writing successfully, and encourage them to draw on their work with their classmate's papers to create standards for their own. Eventually, with your support and feedback, students will reach the point where they can serve as evaluators on their own.

THE QUESTION OF CORRECTNESS

Correctness must be put into its proper place in the composing process. As Lou Kelly (1972) says: "Copyreading is not a part of writing, but a time to consider what you have already written, a time to ask if you have followed all the conventions that will make it easier for your readers to hear what you are saying" (p. 295).

In *Writing: Process and Product,* Susan Miller (1976) describes the value of correctness in mechanics, usage, and spelling as a means of being credible to one's reader, of showing the reader that one knows enough and cares enough to be believed. If writers want to be read, they must put the final manuscript in a form that will not only be comprehensible, but stylistically and grammatically inoffensive.[1]

We subscribe to the philosophy that students have a "right" to their own language (Conference on College Composition and Communication, 1974), but we also feel that students have a right to understand the nature of correctness and a right to the help they need to get their papers into a final stage of correctness. We also think that if standard English is described to students accurately—as a dialect that has gained prestige, not as the *only* proper way to speak and write—then they can make sound decisions for themselves about the value of writing correctly.

Freed from many of its myths and disentangled from the revision stage of the writing process, correctness, our students tell us, "is no big deal." A very large percentage of errors are a result of haste and carelessness, not an inability to use correct English. For the genuine errors—the ones students can't repair based on their existing knowledge—plenty of help is available. We think it is important to make that help available in as convenient a form as possible.

First, help with correctness is available in resource books. We do not advocate using a conventional handbook of grammar and usage as a core text in the writing program, but we think it is useful to have one or several handbooks accessible to students while they are writing. We suggest that our students buy or obtain the use of some sort of spelling, usage, and mechanics guide for writing done outside of class. The teacher's role is not to teach such books cover to cover, but to help students learn to use them, so if they are having trouble with *lay* and *lie* or the spelling of *travelling,* they know how to find the information they need.

Second, help with correctness is available from other students. Peer group work can effectively be extended to the copyreading process. Before a book or article is published, it is proofread many times, by many different eyes, and it is axiomatic that each new copyreader is able to find errors that were previously undetected. At the end of a writing session, we often set aside time for students to exchange papers solely for the purpose of finding errors.

---

[1] Of course, the idea of "caring" can be taken to extremes, made a euphemism for forcing speakers of minority dialects to conform to the dialect of the white, middle-class majority, but the point is valid.

At the same time, it is vital that the novice writer learn to take responsibility for his or her own editing and copyediting. While classmates may help, the writer should not become dependent on them. (Nor should the writer become dependent on the teacher. We absolutely refuse to take on copyreading tasks when students clearly have the skills to do it themselves.)

Students must make a conscious effort, a deliberate choice, to learn how to proofread and to understand the kinds of errors they make. No amount of marginalia and no sequence of grammar exercises will teach students skills unless they care to learn them. Making the writing process authentic—real to the students—can help supply the motivation they need to take a serious interest in correctness. The best way to do that is to provide real, authentic audiences for student writers, the topic we will take up next.

CHAPTER 6

AUDIENCES FOR STUDENT WRITERS

The concept of *audience* has been an important part of theories of rhetoric since their classical beginnings. The impulse to communicate, the desire to share ideas and experiences, is at the heart of the composing process. If writers feel no need to communicate their thoughts to others, the urge to clarify and refine their thoughts is diminished.

Yet despite the antiquity of the concept of audience, texts that purport to teach composition give lip service to it even to this very day. Typically, the texts have very little to say about audience, and even that may not be helpful to the writer. For instance, Frederick Crews, author of the widely used *Random House Handbook* (1977), acknowledges that an essay is "an act of communication—an establishing of a common ground on which two strangers, you and your reader, can agree and meet." Yet he does not describe or offer any writing activities to help the student understand the range and varieties of audiences and the complex demands they place on a writer. Instead, he simply states:

> . . . the proper *audience* of an essay is neither yourself nor your instructor as one unique individual. It is rather a general audience of reasonable people. . . . Your instructor intends to apply . . . standards in reading your work. He or she is, in effect, a stand-in for the anonymous public. By writing for the wider audience that the instructor represents, you can use the course as a workshop for developing your persuasive and communicative skills. (p. 4)

The concept of audience as a generalized group of "reasonable people" is simplistic, yet it persists in much teaching of composition today. Audiences are not, in fact, especially reasonable (though no doubt many of their members are), and they seldom respond in easily predictable patterns. What matters to the novice writer is not this vague, general audience, but the particular audience—quirky, idiosyncratic, immediate, and present—to which he or she must communicate *now*.

Further, we are distrustful of the writing instructor's ability to serve as a "stand-in" for wider audiences. A teacher is a teacher; the students know that and write to the teacher as a result. Gamesmanship—with the teacher pretending to be everyman and everywoman—will simply not work as a way of teaching students to write for audiences. The writing process must be authentic to the student, and this means having students write for authentic audiences.

The work of James Britton (1975) and his colleagues in Great Britain has been useful in helping composition teachers enlarge their view of audience and its function in students' work. He suggests that movement from immature to mature writing involves a developing awareness of audience from readers who are *known* and share a context with the author to those who are more *distant* and *unknown*. "Ideally," he says, "one of the goals is that they [teachers] should, wherever this is possible, produce writers who have developed the capacity to generate their own audiences, which should include those which are large in number and unknown." By "generate," Britton seems to mean both being able to visualize and actually wanting to write for those audiences, a far cry from Crews and his ideas about the teacher as a stand-in audience.

Britton does not exclude the teacher as reader. In fact, he suggests that often in a school setting the teacher may be a member of the audience or the only audience. He suggests that four teacher roles may be appropriate: *teacher as trusted adult, teacher in teacher-student dialogue, teacher in combination professional and personal role,* and *teacher as examiner.* Of these, all but the last involves the teacher as a real person, not just an instructor. Unfortunately, Britton reports, in most of the school writing that he and his colleagues collected in the British schools, the teacher-as-examiner category predominated, suggesting that teachers spend too much time having students use writing to record answers to set questions, too little time asking them to explore fundamental human issues. We are quite certain that the imbalance exists in American schools and colleges as well.

Even if teachers are successful in having themselves serve as human audiences rather than as examiners, the range of audiences must be broadened beyond the instructor. James Moffett (1968) describes learning to write as a decentering process, one in which there is increasing distance between the speaker and the audience. Writers move from reflection to conversation to correspondence to publication, each step involving a larger audience and requiring the writer to imagine or create a picture of the intended audience.

Walker Gibson (1969) also suggests that there is interplay between the voice one uses and the distance between the writer and the audience. He says, "Vocabulary, sentence structure, style vary depending on whether it's an article for students of history or a letter to Jane." He describes characteristics of formal writing in which the distance between writer and audience is great and informal writing in which the distance is small. Formal writing is characterized by the periodic sentence, considerable parallel structure, passive verbs, little use of second person pronouns, and no use of contractions. The informal voice is characterized by loose sentences, little parallelism, active verbs, direct reference to the reader—you, and the use of contractions. However, as Gibson would certainly agree, one does not teach these stylistic features to students and ask them to display the traits in writing. That kind of stylistic imitation could only destroy a writer's natural voice. Instead, writers must have a range of experiences in formal situations and less formal ones that will allow their own tone, style, and voice to emerge.

The process of learning to write for an audience is not so simple or easily come by as Crew's assertion that a student should imagine a reasonable audience, represented by the teacher. The task of the writing teacher is to supply a range of audiences so that the student can develop awareness and the concomitant abilities to shape content, structure, and style to achieve success with a readership.

But therein lies a dilemma. "Of course," many readers will agree, "we want students to write for audiences other than the teacher. But how?" As school and college writing teachers recognize, the composition class is not a real world and it does not, itself, contain a range of audiences. However, it is also evident that most writing teachers do not do as much as they could to find audiences, both classroom audiences and outside audiences, for their students to reach. To that end, this chapter will discuss some practical possibilities. Mirroring the kind of pattern suggested by Britton, Moffett, and Gibson, we will begin with classroom readerships: audiences that are familiar to the student and invite informal writing. We will then widen the circle to discuss other audiences available in the immediate vicinity—within the school or on the college campus. Lastly, we will discuss the community as audience, with "community" taken to represent all outside readerships, whether located in town or thousands of miles away.

AUDIENCES IN THE CLASSROOM

In the previous chapter we showed that treating the writing class as a workshop provides students with opportunities to serve as one another's editors. The line between serving as *editor* and as *reader* is a very fine one, and one doesn't want students to become so completely absorbed in the editing phase of writing that they lose their ability to respond as readers. A real danger of the workshop, peer editing approach is that writers may direct their ideas toward classmate-as-examiner rather than truly develop their papers for broader readerships. In our classes, we make a point of having "reading times," class meetings whose purpose is for the students principally to enjoy one another's work.

ORAL READING.   The day that a final paper is due, we often ask for volunteers to read their papers aloud to the rest of the class. We do not force anyone to read who doesn't want to, but we also watch for those who seem to be quietly tempted to read or who might be willing to have their paper shared if someone else were to read it for them. Early in the course there may only be two or three students eager to have their work read, but as the course progresses and students become more comfortable with one another, the number of volunteer readers increases. The writing workshop also makes some papers of interest to the class because of rumors and hearsay: "I heard that Tom did something funny about the basketball team. Can we hear that one?"

Initially, students seem more willing to read papers that have been written in class than those prepared at home. Because of the limitations, students don't feel that the expectations for in-class writings are as great. The teacher can prepare the class for this kind of activity by collecting a set of papers following an impromptu writing and by reading some—anonymously—to show appreciation of them. By demonstrating that the public reading is safe and by modeling positive reactions the teacher can ease the way to student self-disclosure through writing.

Some teachers we know do the oral presentation through an informal "coffee house" reading. At these specially identified class meetings, students who have completed works read them for the class or for small groups of students. The mood is informal; the tone is one of acceptance. The writer reads; the audience reacts and responds casually. We especially like the coffee house metaphor because it encourages both the teacher and the students to treat novice writers as professionals, not simply as writing students. In effect, what is read is perceived and reacted to as literature, not as a student composition or theme.

DISPLAYS AND ONE-OF-A-KIND PUBLICATIONS.   The oral reading offers a safe beginning for audience reactions because the actual paper never leaves the hands of the writer (or it is only seen by one other person, the public reader). Thus matters of mechanics, form, and penmanship are relevant only as they affect the reader's ability to recode the writing into speech. Many problems with surface correctness can thus be ignored for the moment.

However, as part of expanding the circle of audiences, students must come to realize that form and mechanics are also an important part of the writing process. Displaying student work is one way of introducing this concern for the audience of peers.

Skill at the use of display space seems to decrease proportionally with the increasing grade level of the teacher. Elementary school bulletin boards are usually jammed with student work. In high school the boards are often blank or used only occasionally. In colleges, the bulletin boards—if they exist in the classroom at all—are covered with announcements of rock concerts and advertisements for magazines, not with student writing.

More ought to be done with displaying student writing at the upper levels. It may be that college instructors are unwilling or unable to create displays that are left on the board after class ends, and high school teachers may not have their own assigned classrooms, making cultivation of the bulletin boards difficult. Still, both school and college teachers can create many kinds of temporary displays. Instead of the coffee house reading the teacher might set up a kind of reading fair, with final copies of papers tacked to the board or even taped to the schoolroom walls for a class period. One high school teacher we know even strings clothesline in her classroom and has her students hang their writing out "to dry" with clothespins.

In creating these kinds of displays, we have found it useful for writers to leave out (or up) blank sheets of paper for comments. During the class period the students circulate around the room, reading as many papers as they can, offering comments on the blank sheets. Often exchanges will take place between commentators, with one reader disagreeing with another about a response to a piece. Obviously, such disagreement is extremely valuable to the writer, helping him or her much more than the imagined responses of the mythical audience of reasonable people.

"One-of-a-kind" publications are a step beyond the classroom display. Students prepare their final copy as if it were being published. Then they may bind it as a short book, put it in a notebook and illustrate it, or carefully type copy that looks printed. As we remind students, "You have put a lot of effort into writing something that reads well, that says what you want it to say. Now preserve it in a form that is attractive to readers." In another book, *Gifts of Writing,* we have outlined numerous one-of-a-kind publications such as folding books, leaflets, scrolls, quartos and folios, hand-bound books, and books with sewn signatures (Judy and Judy, 1980). Although art and craft work is involved (work that some high school and college teachers think belongs in the elementary grades) we have found that students at all levels, from pre-school through graduate school delight in presenting their work to an audience in this way.

CLASS PUBLICATIONS.   One of the most successful ways we have found for providing students with an audience is the class magazine. The students serve as both editors and readers of the magazine, and it gives something tangible to them to take outside class, thus bridging the gap between the writing classroom and the real world. Magazines can be produced very inexpensively through the use of ditto or mimeograph processes; but, if the budget permits, they can be done through photocopying or offset printing as well.

The frequency of publishing class magazines in a writing course depends on several variables: the length of the course, the number of students in your classes, the relative availability of paper and copy services. In a ten week course, we have found that producing a single quality magazine as a culminating project is practical. In a sixteen week term, we have had students do two: one at midterm and the other at the end of the course. We have also had students do magazines as small group projects, leading to the production of a half dozen or more magazines during a term, and once, as part of a young writer's workshop, we led seventy junior high students in the production of fourteen—count 'em—dittoed magazines during a single Saturday morning session.

In schools where supplies are short, shorter publications than the full magazine can be explored. For example, in one school where we have taught, students in a writing course prepared a series of broadsheets or fliers, two-sided, 8½ × 14 inch mimeographed sheets containing all the student writing we could possibly cram onto them. Published weekly, this writing leaflet could be distributed to every student in the school, yet consumed less than a ream of paper per week.

To create a magazine, we ask students to select the best writing they have done in recent weeks and to revise it one last time. We advise them to take into consideration the critiques and responses they have previously received. Sometimes papers go through minor changes at this stage; sometimes the students, having had a chance to ruminate on their compositions for a period of time, decide to redo the paper entirely, changing structure, adding sections, deleting material, or possibly even combining papers on related topics. Knowing that the paper will be published seems to make a great difference to the students, even if the audience will just be their classmates, many of whom have already read the paper.

When the papers have been revised, the students bring the drafts to class and we break the class into three groups: a proofreading group, a table-of-contents group, and a design/production group. We ask that each paper be proofread two more times to check all matters of correctness. Students are asked to bring handbooks and dictionaries to class and to ask questions if they are unsure of usage or mechanics. We emphasize that at this publication stage the time has come to eradicate errors.

The responsibility of the table-of-contents group is to "orchestrate" everyone's writings. Each writer provides the group with the title of his or her piece and a synopsis. The table-of-contents group then creates categories or subheadings into which the papers fall and decides on a sequence. Though the task may seem to be a simple one, this group almost always ends up in very long, animated discussions. The magazine, we remind them, should not merely be a collection of papers stapled together. It should have direction, flow, and a sense of purpose. The table-of-contents group also is responsible for choosing a title for the magazine and/or starting its overall theme.

The duties of the design/production group will vary depending on the medium of duplicating. For example, if the magazine is to be printed on ditto masters, every student in the class can take responsibility for cutting his or her own master—making a clean, perfect final copy and possibly adding embellishments or artwork. Or the design group can hold every student responsible for creating final copy in class or at home, handwritten or typed, and then have the class artists add decorative material. If mimeograph is the medium, the stencils usually have to be cut by someone outside the class, perhaps a school secretary or students in a business education class. Then the stencils are returned to the design group; using a simple light table and special styli, it prepares the art and graphic material.

The design/production group works closely with the table-of-contents group to make the design of the magazine fit the contents. When the master copies have been prepared, they are sent off to the mimeograph room or duplicating service for actual production.

When the completed books arrive, students open them up and read them, starting with their own stories, essays, or poems, then moving on to those of other members of the class. Even though the students have read or worked with many of the pieces, they do not seem to mind reading them again. Comments spontaneously erupt around the room, and we gladly give over a class period to reading.

We have also asked students to make more formal kinds of responses to the published magazines. For example, we have asked that students write letters on pieces they particularly enjoyed or pieces with which they disagreed. We stress that at this point the purpose in writing is not to tell the author how to improve the paper but to give an honest human reaction—an audience reaction.

Sometimes we will organize the class so to guarantee that each author will receive two or three responses (this is to overcome the problem that frequently one or two pieces will attract everyone's attention). A good compromise strategy is for each person to write a letter to an author assigned by the teacher, then to write a letter to an author of his or her choice.

We have also used these booklets and magazines as part of "assigned reading" for the course, discussing the pieces just as one would selections in a literature anthology. We raise some of the following questions for discussion:

Which of the stories/essays/poems had particular impact on you and why?

Were there particular events, experiences, ideas, and beliefs represented in these papers that were similar to your own? In what ways were they similar? How were they different?

Were there events, ideas, and beliefs that ran counter to your own experiences and ideas? How? Describe them.

How do the authors use examples and illustrations to support their ideas and illustrate their experiences?

Usually the discussion helps to confirm the students' sense of the successful parts of their own writing and creates an impulse to share the writing with a broader audience. In the schools, this sharing may often be done with parents. In college it will often involve roommates and friends. In both instances, the desire to share a completed classroom magazine provides a transition to other, broader audiences.

AUDIENCES AROUND THE SCHOOL

If the budget will stand it, we usually try to run off one extra copy of the classroom magazine for each member of the class, thus providing a copy to give to others. Some teachers arrange to have copies put on reserve or on public display in the library, thus generating an expanded readership for the publication. Consequently, the classroom magazine is not strictly limited to the room where it was created. The school or campus offers other possibilities for readership as well.

EXISTING SCHOOL PUBLICATIONS. Every school or college has at least one and probably several outlets for student writing, and teachers should familiarize themselves with these publications (and get to know their faculty advisors). Some colleges have literally dozens of small magazines and monographs, funded at levels that range from shoestring to substantial investment. Many high schools have at least one literary magazine, and often the school newspaper will publish poetry and fiction as well as news stories and feature articles. It brings a strong element of authenticity to the writing process, for the teacher can describe such audiences and publication possibilities early in the course, inviting students to write for publication from the very beginning.

CREATING A SCHOOL PUBLICATION. Alas, in some schools and colleges, the publications are controlled by small special interest groups, a self-selected few who fancy themselves the literary elite. It is tough for outsiders to break into the circle. Too, in many schools (particularly high schools) the faculty advisors of the standard publications are concerned not with developing writers, but with publishing what strikes them as out-standing, mature work. Thus the youngster who has never published, whose style is vigorous but unpolished, whose syntax is not quite on a par with that of the *Atlantic* (or the *Scholastic* magazine award winners), is excluded from publication.

If that is the case, the writing instructor may wish to sponsor alternative publications. It is not terribly difficult for a teacher who has a good idea for a publication to get outside funding and support. Banks, restaurants, record shops, clothing stores and the like seem willing enough to purchase ads in magazines directed precisely toward their young adult clientele. Further, offset printing technology allows one to produce a quality magazine or jour-nal relatively inexpensively. If the school-sponsored publications are closed to your students, start your own. (For a useful article on ways and means of starting a publishing company with your students, see John Marshall Carter, "Publish or Perish: Inspiration and Reward" [1979].) Writing instructors familiar with *Foxfire* magazine, a student-written journal of folk culture that began in Rabun Gap, Georgia, may be interested in knowing that it has over two hundred successful imitators, most of them privately financed.

ORAL READINGS/DRAMATIC PRESENTATIONS. Marvin Zimmerman (1979), the English chair at Little Rock Parkview High School, has observed that English teachers can successfully form liaisons with speech/drama teachers to encourage the "publication" of student work. Members of a speech or drama class might simply do well-prepared oral readings of pieces written in English. More elaborately, students from both classes might col-laborate to do shows based on student writing, possibly with music and slide photographs. It has always seemed to us unfortunate that so many of the plays presented in school and college are not written by the students them-selves. While we can appreciate that having a play by a name author will help to fill auditorium seats, we would much rather watch a night of student-written one-act plays than sit through an amateurish performance of a heavyweight Pulitzer Prize drama or a rerun of last year's successful Broadway musical sung and danced by youngsters who are not very good at either.

CAMPUS RADIO/TELEVISION. Most college campuses have their own closed circuit radio and television stations, and some even have commercial stations that broadcast into the community. In the high schools, the public address system often serves as a kind of radio station for the school. Closed circuit television can be broadcast into many schoolrooms, and, in some instances, can be hooked into local cable television as well. The possibilities for media production of student writing are exciting.

YOUNG WRITERS' WORKSHOPS. In what has almost reached fad proportions, many schools are sponsoring workshops for young writers. Formats vary widely. Sometimes the young writers come to the workshop with their final drafts in hand, and the day is spent sharing their work with other students. Other times a poet or novelist will attend, his or her way paid by a state arts council, to meet with young writers and to make suggestions about their work. We have sponsored many workshops in Mt. Pleasant and East Lansing, Michigan, where students do their writing at the workshop under the guidance of undergraduate prospective teachers, with the results of the workshop gathered into a booklet and published.

WRITERS' CLUBS. Closely related in principle to the young authors' workshop, the writer's club offers an opportunity for sustained growth and development of student writers. Of course, it is important to insure that the club is open to all students and that it actively solicits membership from the entire student body. It serves no great need if, like some conventional literary magazines, the club becomes the private hangout of a select few budding Hemingways.

AUDIENCES IN THE COMMUNITY
Locating a readership for student writing beyond the school or campus perimeter is perhaps the most difficult part of providing authentic audiences for the writing class. Yet the possibilities that exist have seldom been fully exploited.

WRITING TO OTHER SCHOOLS. Many writing instructors attend state or national conventions where they frequently meet teachers with common interests. Paper exchanges are easily set up between schools or classes, with the price of postage all that is required to move a batch of papers from one part of the state or country to another. The recipients of the papers read them, talk about them, and write back reactions, following guidelines established beforehand by the cooperating teachers.

Writing to peers in other schools makes the transition from writing to a "known" to an essentially "unknown" audience. At the same time, because they have many beliefs and interests in common with their readers, student writers do not need to make radical changes in their content and style.

What to write about? Classes we know of participating in exchanges have chosen some of the following topics:

A description of some aspects of high school or college life. Dorm food and cafeteria cooking are universal topics, as are social events, athletics, student rights and government.

Sharing hobbies and skills: how to tie flies, write poetry, fix a bicycle, lose weight, win a boxing match.

Pure storytelling: experiences and events in the life of the writer.

Geographical descriptions, especially if the students live in dramatically different climates.

Movie and television reviews.

LETTERS. An infinite range of audiences is available to the letter writer, from known readers who welcome informal writing to unknown readers in formal situations. Students can write everyone from school officials to administrators of policies in education, industry, and business. They can write to artists, musicians, poets, and actors to offer adulation or criticism. They can write on issues of immediate concern or those of long-standing interest.

One useful letter writing activity is for students to write two or more letters on the same topic to two or more people. Thus they might write to their mother and a close friend about a personal problem; to a professor, the university president, and the state governor about a campus issue; to a store manager and his/her advertising agency about goods, services, and advertising. In writing these letters, students are given an unusual opportunity to compare the needs and requirements of different audiences.

We do not encourage instructors to use dummy run activities just to get students to experiment with voice, style, and persona. However, letter writing does give the writer an opportunity to alter the self he or she commits to paper. Certainly, writing multiple letters allows the writer to see the various ways of presenting content (and, in fact, how content differs) from one writing situation to another.

COMMUNITY PUBLICATIONS. It is surprisingly easy for students who are willing to do careful work to get their writing published in local newspapers and magazines. While the press is selective in what it chooses to use, most editors confess that they are constantly on the lookout for new ideas and materials to fill their pages. (To a newspaper editor, tomorrow's edition must sometimes seem as frightening as a blank sheet of paper to a novice writer.) There is space to fill, and there is no reason why student writers of all ages cannot help fill it.

The letters-to-the-editor page, of course, provides a good starting point. Our only suggestion here is that teachers do not send class sets of letters to the editor. Most editors don't have time to sift through thirty or more "compositions" on a topic and may rightly feel imposed upon if asked to. We suggest that writing a letter to the editor be offered as a course option, and that the teacher remind students of the possibilities. Thus if a current issue or problem invoke's one student's curiosity, the teacher can suggest that he or she develop the idea for the paper.

There are also opportunities to publish longer, more sustained pieces. Most papers and local magazines are on the lookout for feature articles on a variety of topics: school doings, local characters, community events, and so on. Sometimes the paper will dispatch a reporter to cover something of interest, but often only the big news items receive coverage. A well-developed student piece on an interesting, but less important matter stands a good change of being accepted.

The teacher wanting to promote this kind of writing might confer first with the editor to check on possibilities. However, often the editor will be noncommittal, not wishing either to encourage a flood of bad writing or to get into a position of having to accept something. We think it works better for the teacher to serve as a kind of broker or agent, taking a completed piece of writing to the editor and asking for a reading of it.

In addition, many community newspapers are willing to set aside a page every week or month for student writing, provided, once again, that they can be assured of its quality. When the writing teacher has gained the confidence of the editor, it is possible for the writing class to reach a wide audience, at absolutely no cost to the school, through the community publication.

COMMUNITY RADIO/TV.   All radio stations are required by the Federal Communications Commission to give over a certain amount of air time to public service broadcasting. The all-music stations, in particular, find filling this time a bit of a chore and they often use network supplied blurbs or materials supplied by the advertising council. A composition teacher in search of audiences might contact local stations to inquire about the use of this time for young people's writing. A "youth forum" for example, with young people reading papers on current issues would qualify as an FCC public service program, as would one that featured student creative writing.

Television time is somewhat harder to come by because of the tremendous expenses involved in producing even simple television programs. However, the advent of cable television has created new possibilities for the writing teacher. FCC regulations require each cable outlet provide support for one or more community cable channels. Essentially, these are open channels, and anything a community member wants to show over them must, by law, be shown. Most cable corporations have modest studios for making tapes and putting on live performances and, if they do not, they certainly can play videotapes recorded at school. Again a wide range possible programs exists, from simple readings of students writing to dramatized reader's theater productions of short stories.

CIVIC PERFORMANCES. Many communities and schools sponsor arts festivals or arts weeks in which a number of cultural events take place. Why not a night honoring the achievements of student writers? Conducting such an evening need not be terribly expensive, and it proves relatively easy to turn out a large and interested crowd to hear young authors reading their own works.

The writing teacher should also be alert to civic events and celebrations: centennials and sesquicentennials, the opening of a museum, holidays. The people in charge of such events might welcome student-written materials ranging from historical studies to feature pieces, and heaven knows that these kinds of events need an infusion of good, lively writing.

Civic and service clubs might provide another outlet, either for a performance of student writing or writing prepared to serve a particular group's needs.

CONTESTS. Writing awards and contests are controversial among writing instructors. On the one hand, having students write for contests or submit work for an award stimulates interest and encourages young writers to think about outside audiences. On the other hand, the motivation for writing—to win a prize or award—is rather arbitrary, divorced from the real reasons most people write: to communicate something to another person. Contests can also induce false competitiveness in a writing class. Although an award may bestow prestige on the winner, it may cast a negative pall over the rest of the class members who are losers—or, at least, not winners.

We rather like the attitude toward contests demonstrated by the organizers of the Youth Talent Awards of the Lansing, Michigan, *State Journal.* Cash prizes are given to the best-of-classification winners, and all entrants are eligible to win first, second, third prize, and honorable mention ribbons. The organizers place no limit on the number of ribbons in each category, so, in effect, any student who writes well stands a good chance of earning a prize. Such a liberal policy, we think, helps to eliminate many of the negative factors associated with contests.

A directory of selected national writing contests and awards is given in Appendix B, and the writing teacher may want to write to the addresses given to find information on this year's contest deadlines. Not listed in the appendix are the hundreds of state, local, and campus awards and contests students may enter. To find further information on these, write to your local or state arts council.

WRITING FOR PUBLICATION. After students have had experience writing for a variety of audiences you provided and have developed some sophistication in adjusting their content, style, and tone, you might want to offer them the option of writing for a larger unknown audience and submitting their writing for publication.

The odds against getting something published in a commercial, national magazine are rather high, and you should warn your students that rejection is much more likely than acceptance. But with that warning in mind, students often enjoy writing for submission to a well-known publication. A rejection slip—even a form rejection—can be a prestige item to show about the class. Sometimes, knowing that the author is a young person, an editor will take time to write a personal note of advice or encouragement.

The Writer's Handbook and *Literary Market Place* list places to publish fiction, nonfiction, poetry, humor and drama. The annotations in these directories suggest the kinds of topics the editors see as appropriate, and many magazines ask for articles that are within the range of experience of school and college students. A list of magazines that currently encourage or accept writing from young people or about young adult interests is provided in Appendix B.

Students should not write for magazines based on an annotation in a publication directory alone. We suggest that the instructor bring copies of the magazine to class or have the students supply back issues. Ask students to consider answers to some of the following questions:

What is the age of the audience for this magazine?

How specialized are the articles?

Do the readers seem to know much about the subject already? Is the magazine general, offering an overview, or is it somewhat technical, expecting the readers to know a great deal about the subject before they begin?

The most important question to ask relates not so much to the audience as to the students themselves:

Given what you know about this audience, what do you have to tell it? What special skills, knowledge, or experiences might you share?

Writing for audiences is not a cure-all for composition problems. It will not make students write better than they are capable of writing; it will not make all their usage and spelling errors go away. But in our experience teaching both school and college writing courses, nothing a teacher can do will bring more interest, enthusiasm, and authenticity to the class than supplying an honest, interested audience.

CHAPTER 7

DESIGNS FOR WRITING COURSES

To this point we have described the teaching of writing by means of individual assignments or activities. We have discussed ways and means of making writing experiences complete in themselves and meaningful to the student writer. And there is no question that individual writing experiences must be at the very center of a writing program. But the word "program" itself implies a sequencing or ordering of instruction so that student growth takes place as systematically as possible.

In too many courses the writing is required sporadically, and the relationship between assignments seems random. Under some theme-a-week plans, for example, the teacher's main goal seems to be coming up with something—*anything*—for the students to write about. What happens on one Theme Friday (or Tuesday or Thursday) shows no connection with what preceded or what will follow. (The very popular "directories" of composition topics—*1001 Writing Ideas* or *Composition Starters for All Situations*—show the appeal of this approach. One simply scans the list to find a topic that may intrigue the students.)

Sometimes the students must come up with the topic: "Write about whatever interests you." Although that "assignment" may seem to be a way of drawing out students' personal experiences, it may leave them operating out of a vacuum (wishing, perhaps, that *they* owned a copy of *1001 Writing Ideas.*)

Often writing assignments grow from the need for teachers to find novelty for their students instead of from the students' needs as writers; in that case, the writing program becomes a series of "shocking" or clever stimuli, followed by whatever writing has been provoked in students.

While one can make too much of the need for structure and sequence, we believe every teacher ought to begin his or her writing course with some kind of sensible developmental plan in mind, even if it is a plan that will be revised and altered. It should be concerned with assessing students' strengths and weaknesses as writers (something we will discuss in the next chapter), and it should be aimed at creating a sequence of flow of classroom activities that will genuinely promote student growth in writing along the lines that teachers and students see as important.

Curiously, the professional literature is thin on the topic of writing course design. Although this year's crop of journal articles will undoubtedly contain hundreds of articles on successful writing topics and an equal number on ways and means of assessing student themes, we will be surprised if more than a dozen will discuss the intricacies of course design and, of those, many will be of the "unsolicited testimonial" type, in which the writer talks about the nuts and bolts of a specific course that seemed successful but does not describe the underlying principles leading to creation of the course. By default, course design often falls to the writers of school and college textbooks.

We are frankly appalled at the amount of time college curriculum committees give over to the adoption of basic textbooks while ignoring the topic of course design. The discussions are agonizing and apparently endless as instructors talk about the merits and deficiencies of particular texts. These committees obviously know that in a very high percentage of college courses the text itself becomes the course. Oh, the instructor may rearrange the order of chapters, but the basic assumptions of the text writer become those of the instructor and of the course. The prevalence of this adoption syndrome is well documented by the flood of writing books on the college text market. Every year sees publishers introducing dozens of new texts, and it is no secret that both the publishers and authors lust after the massive adoptions that will make a book a best seller, one that can be revised many times over a period of years, supplying a steady, predictable income.

The situation is different, but no better, in the schools. There, in fact, the problem is compounded by the prevalence of textbook series and multicomponent programs. Adoption may involve a kindergarten through twelfth grade set of textbooks, or, at the very least, a six-or seven-year junior high/senior high program. Although one can understand the appeal of adopting a series of materials—they do, in a sense, guarantee a kind of uniformity and consistency among teachers and grade levels—the common tendency is for the adopted book to become the course, to become the program. On a number of occasions we have had the opportunity to review school curriculum guides where the stated objectives and the sequence of instruction were borrowed directly from the adopted texts.

Our remark here should not be construed as "anti-textbook." There are some good school and college texts on the market, and we will refer to several elsewhere in the chapter. But good texts should complement a course design developed by the instructor; they should not create it. Further, we think teachers should resist the tendency to let programs remain static for the period of adoption of a book. Every time one teaches a writing course the design ought to be tailor-made for the students. While one may find a good book that can be used over and over again, the fine details of the course ought to evolve and be adapted to student needs, independently of the text itself.

In this chapter we will fill what seems to us a gap in the professional literature by presenting a survey and critique of composition course designs. For our data, we reviewed the professional literature that does exist, studied dozens of school and college textbooks, and conducted an informal survey of writing instructors in all parts of the country. (Their names are listed on the Acknowledgments page.) We do not claim that our survey is exhaustive. Nor is our presentation of the findings intended to be objective. We will describe, first, three models that exist in a great many schools and colleges and that, we think, have outlived their usefulness. We will then offer six contemporary models for writing courses that we think are both successful and in keeping with the principles advanced in this book.

THREE CONVENTIONAL MODELS: A CRITIQUE

THE BASIC SKILLS APPROACH. Unquestionably, this is the most common plan for organizing a writing course. The rationale is clearly explained in a book somewhat presumptuously titled, *The Right Book,* by Hilson and Kramer (1980):

> *It is our belief that you should not be lied to. Writing is hard work. If you are going to build a doghouse, you are in tough shape if you do not have a hammer and nails. In* The Right Book, *it is our intention to give you that hammer and those nails so that by the time you have worked your way through this text, you will be able to construct well-designed essays.* (p. vi)

The "hammer and nails" the authors present are, predictably, the elements of formal grammar and usage as well as some formulas for structured essays, all put together in a fill-in-the-blanks workbook. The book thus nicely illustrates the two basic assumptions of the skills approach:

1. That writing can be broken down into small parts—basic skills.
2. That the skills can be learned, one at a time, then put together when one writes whole essays.

We have discussed the fallacies behind those two assumptions elsewhere, but it is important to note once again that with written composition, the whole is invariably greater than the sum of the parts, and it is *wholes* that students must write, not practice fragments. Yet, the typical basic skills course begins with small fragments of language, *words,* teaches their names and functions (parts-of-speech grammar), then moves on to longer language fragments, *sentences* and *paragraphs*, before taking up whole compositions.

It is generally believed by the press and the public that the basic skills approach is not widely practiced in the schools today, that getting away from basics is responsible for the writing deficiencies of young people. We wish they were right about the "getting away" part. We find that in most schools and colleges the basics never left, and if any particular instructional method is responsible for students' bad writing, it is the basic skills approach. The "hammer and nails" metaphor is an ancient one, and it has been tried but not found true. We think its demise is long overdue.

THE EXPOSITORY RHETORIC APPROACH. Often combined with a basic skills approach, this method shows students the patterns of completed, successful compositions. It generally begins with an explication of paragraph structure, including topic or thesis sentence, development, and concluding or clincher statement. The students learn a variety of methods of paragraph and/or essay development; the most common forms taught include *process analysis, thesis and support, division and classification, comparison and contrast, definition,* and *cause and effect.* The expository rhetoric course may often conclude with some elementary lessons in style, with a focus on sentence variation.

Like the basic skills approach, this one teaches language skills through isolated practice. Here, for example, is a practice assignment from a current college rhetoric text, James Raymond's *Writing (Is an Unnatural Act)* (1980):

> Write a comparison and contrast paper that your classmates would find interesting and informative. (p. 34)

We frankly find the writing of comparison and contrast papers an unnatural act. Few writers set out deliberately to use one rhetorical structure or another, and it seems to us singularly unhelpful to require students to do so. Note, for example, how the concern for mastering the rhetorical process distorts the writing process in the author's follow-up instructions:

1. *Choose a pair of subjects that have enough common characteristics and enough differences to generate a paper.*
2. *Study the subjects until you can find at least three categories of comparison.*
3. *Make notes about similarities and differences in each category.*
4. *Outline the body of the paper (see p. 94) and write it.*
5. *Add an introduction (p. 164) and a conclusion (see p. 130).*
6. *Revise and edit (see Chapters Six and Seven)*

(p. 34)

In that six-item list, the quest for points of comparison predominates, so much so that the selection of topic is dictated by whether or not it lends itself to this particular rhetorical treatment, and the search for materials ends just as soon as the student can find three comparable points. Any sense of genuine purpose for this composition is lost (even though the students are told, almost as an afterthought, to make it "interesting and informative" for their classmates).

We've read many hundreds of papers produced by the rhetorical expository approach and find them generally wooden and dull. Concern for technique eclipses the content, and students perform, not like writers, but as imitators of other writers.

LITERARY MODELS APPROACH. Imitation is a problem with this approach as well, though its proponents see that as its strong point. As its title implies, the literary models method provides students with examples of good writing and asks them to use the same techniques in their own work. In some courses, the imitation is quite slavish, with students following "master" works—usually essays—point by point. More commonly, the novice writer studies the model and then loosely applies the techniques to his or her own work.

Still, to our mind, almost any form of direct imitation leads to a distortion of the writing process. Note the details of this assignment from Clayes, Spencer, and Stanford's *Contexts for Composition* (1976):

> Write a description of an event (an accident, a fire, a lost child) or a place (a mountain or sea in storm, a desert, a city street, an airport, bus or train station) first with the disciplined reporting of concrete details of [Alexander] Leighton's style, then employing some of the more elaborate devices and personal response of [James] Baldwin's style or the wit of Eleanor Clark's. (p. 268)

We find this exercise far beyond the capabilities of the college freshmen for whom it is intended, calling for an understanding of the prose styles of three authors and the ability to apply that understanding to one's own writing, whether a description of a fire or a train station. Very few professional writers are willing to tinker with their own style in this way, and most argue, sensibly, that a writer should concentrate on letting style reflect his or her own unique perceptions and observations. Like the expository rhetoric approach, this one detracts from content and the student's ability to find and synthesize material, all for the sake of surface appearance.

The literary models approach is particularly popular in college programs, in part because it satisfies a latent desire on the part of many freshman writing instructors to deal with literature. Many of them are trained primarily to teach literature and are not enthusiastic about composition. When they take a literary models approach, they are free to discuss the form and style of great writers, not just that of freshmen. This, in turn, can create a problem of course balance, and a number of colleges have actually banned literary readers from the writing course on the grounds that instructors abuse them, teaching literature to the exclusion of writing.

TOWARD A SYNTHESIS OF APPROACHES: THE DANGERS

In this brief critique we have attempted to describe the three conventional approaches as discrete entities. In fact, one often finds writing courses in schools and colleges that combine elements of all three. Thus the basic skills method, with its special emphasis on grammar, flows into the expository rhetoric approach, where essay construction is at the center of concern. Literary models can be used to demonstrate all facets of a course from sentence construction to form and style.

We agree with the impulse that suggests a combination of methods is probably better than reliance on a single approach. Unfortunately, in a great many writing programs the synthesis draws on the very worst aspects of all three, leading to writing courses far removed from the principles we have suggested in this book. Perhaps most dangerous is that many courses and programs seems to represent a pick-and-choose approach, one without a central overriding philosophy. The components selected may bear no relationship to one another, and one can find inconsistencies in pedagogy within a single course.

For example, a guide for an upper-level high school composition course lists the following as paragraph skills:

Narrating a simple personal experience through a single paragraph.

Writing a paragraph in which the supporting details are:
1. in chronological order
2. in spatial order
3. in order of importance

Developing a paragraph in which a procedure is explained.

Although these skills obviously come out of a rhetorical expository approach, we are at a loss to see why they are presented in this order or why these three particular aspects of the paragraph have been selected. Similarly, in reviewing a section on vocabulary, we find ourselves unable to find the underlying rationale for these areas of study:

Words from special areas and jobs.

Words from his [the student's] reading.

Synonyms, antonyms, homonyms.

Transition words.

A word as more than one part of speech.

Figurative language—similies, metaphors, personification, alliteration, onomatopoeia, allusion, interrogation, euphemism, and assonance.

Words with emotive force.

Slang and/or formal usage when needed.

Words for their denotation or connotation.

Dictionary at appropriate reading level.

Further along in this chapter we will describe a course that represents a successful synthesis of various approaches. The conventional models—basic skills, expository rhetoric, and literary models—do not offer a great deal of hope for a solid synthesis. To find that possibility, one needs to look to a series of contemporary writing course models that reject the older imitation-and-drill pedagogy and look to the writer and the writing process for their underlying rationale and coherence.

CONTEMPORARY MODELS FOR WRITING COURSES

WRITING AS PROCESS. The person most responsible for popularizing a writing process approach to the composition course is Donald Murray of the University of New Hampshire (1978, 1979), though much of the early work in this area was done by Wallace Douglas (1963) of Northwestern University, who, in turn, credits Porter Perrin of Colgate University and his teaching techniques developed in the 1930s and 1940s. In simplest terms, this method organizes the program around the stages of the writing process itself.

Murray describes the process in three stages: *rehearsing* (which involves gathering data and making preliminary plans for what one is going to say), *drafting,* and *revising.* He visualizes the act of writing as a continuing cycle with the writer *collecting* information, *connecting* bits and parts to create a whole, *writing,* and *reading* what has been written.

Murray has given workshops on his method all over the country, and one of his students has shown how he applies the method in his own teaching at Oxbow High School in Bradford, Vermont. When he makes an assignment, Joseph Moore (1978) holds a "writing week," with each day devoted to one phase or aspect of the writing process.

Monday begins with idea gathering, Murray's *rehearsing, collecting,* and *connecting:*

> *Students discuss and jot down topics which might interest them. Each student then chooses one of these topics and begins writing notes or lists*

of information, ideas, feelings, or recollections related to that topic. Once these notes are compiled, and the students are convinced they know enough about the topic, they begin the first draft. The paper may be primarily descriptive, narrative, persuasive, or any other non-fiction type. Often the student isn't even aware what "type" of paper it is. (p. 39)

The students then begin writing, first silently, later with an opportunity to raise questions of fellow students or the teacher.

Tuesday is drafting day. The students continue to write, refining their notes, jottings, and preliminary efforts from Monday into solid drafts. Moore circulates around the room coaching, advising, assisting. The students are also urged to share rough drafts with one another to solicit a response.

Wednesday centers on the reading of drafts. Moore has his students sit in a large circle and pass papers around. The reading is silent, though occasionally students may make specific comments to one another. "The primary focus in this class is perceptive reading; our secondary aim is positive, specific commentary." For Wednesday night homework, each student takes home somebody else's essay for commentary:

The first part of the evaluation is a brief paragraph in which the evaluators respond as readers, not as a substitute English teacher. . . . In the second part, the evaluator lists ten specific strengths in the essay. . . . Finally, the student evaluator makes two specific suggestions— only two. (p. 40)

On Thursday, the written comments are returned to the students, who set about writing their revisions, absorbing the praise, and operating on the suggestions made by the readers.

On Friday, three or four of the newly revised papers are discussed by the class as a whole under the careful guidance of the instructor. Here the analysis is detailed, with commentary focused on both the students' reactions to the paper and their suggestions for additional improvement. For Friday homework, the students are expected to revise and polish their work into its final form. The completed essays go into the student's file for subsequent evaluation by the teacher.

We find a great deal of appeal in the kind of approach suggested by Murray and Moore. This is clearly a learn-to-write-by-writing method, with almost no use of basic skills or rhetorical expository instruction. The students write from their own experience, so that gathering and collecting material is not difficult, and the students always have something to say. We approve, too, of the emphasis on peer reading and feedback of the teacher's unobtrusive role as writing coach.

Yet despite our commitment to teaching writing-as-process, we do not use the process model as a method of organizing our own courses. For one thing, we are edgy about the way in which topics are developed, with the students simply brainstorming for topics and drawing exclusively on past personal experiences. There are many ways for the teacher to provide starting points for writing, leading the class not only to explore past experience, but to move into new areas.

There is also a regimentation to the process approach that concerns us, and we prefer a less formal writing workshop method where students do not always draft, revise, edit at the same time. We fear that having the students all do the same steps on the same days not only cramps writing styles but can lead to unnecessary breaks in the flow of the writing process. For example, in Murray's book on the process approach, *A Writer Teaches Writing* (1968), he has students bring in lists of "specifics" on one day and hone those specifics down to a smaller list the next, with both tasks done independently of drafting a paper. As important as it is to have students experience the phases of the writing process, we think that this kind of structuring breaks up the organic unity of the writing act.

We find it useful to incorporate the concept of writing-as-process within one or more of the models that follow. At the same time, we know many, many teachers who find the process method a practical, manageable way of organizing the writing program. By following the stages in order, the teacher can concentrate on helping students with those phases where they are least successful. Peer evaluation and editing is built in at several points in the program and, as a result, the teacher's theme correcting burden is lightened. The writing as process approach has many advantages, and readers of this book may well want to experiment with it.

PERCEPTUAL APPROACH. It is axiomatic among writers and teachers of writing that the quality of one's perceptions directly affects the quality of his or her writing. To write well, one must observe carefully, absorbing details, selecting among them, getting them down on paper. It is also axiomatic that without support, encouragement, and practice, people's sensibilities tend to become dulled so that they live in a world without actually seeing or perceiving it carefully. The perceptual approach tries to remedy that by teaching—or, more accurately, by fostering—observation of the world.

The roots of this approach run deep in American education. In the mid-nineteenth century, for example, many elementary and secondary school teachers presented their students with "object lessons" involving observation of the natural world followed by conversation and/or writing. Thus children might examine a ball, a jacknife, or a stuffed animal, or even go out in nature to examine trees, flowers, lakes and ponds. The naturalist Louis Agassiz was notorious among university students of that period for having students literally spend days in a laboratory studying a specimen until they discovered—perceived—all there was to learn about it.

When applied to writing instruction, the perceptual approach is easily abused. Obviously, one cannot instruct people in how to see; one can merely point out that there is a world to be observed and encourage people to see it. Equally important, there is no one-to-one correspondence between perception and writing. That is, one does not merely *transcribe* perceptions; the writer must synthesize them with his or her past experiences and make something of them. Mere listing of perceptions can create intolerably dull themes (as many of the nineteenth-century object teachers discovered).

In our judgment, far and away the best model of the perceptual approach is presented in a college textbook, *Here and Now,* by Fred Morgan (1979). In the Preface he explains:

> *Good thinking and writing cannot grow out of second-hand material, but must be firmly rooted in the ability of students to observe and interpret for themselves.*

In this respect, Morgan's is like Murray's process approach, relying on material that the writer has in his or her mind. But unlike Murray, Morgan sets about helping students find—perceive—that material systematically. His sequence of writing projects thus aims at developing perceptual skills:

> *. . . students are encouraged to begin at the beginning by examining their own surroundings. . . . They start with simple objects and progress toward complex ones, but without departing from first-hand observation and experience.*

The flow of simple to complex is shown in the sequence of chapters in the book, a sequence that can serve very nicely as a course outline:

Enjoying Your Senses
Employing Your Senses
Being Aware of Surroundings
Observing a Scene
Getting the Feel of Action
Observing a Person
Perceiving Emotional Attitudes
Estimating a Person
Identifying With a Person
Perceiving a Relationship
Looking at Yourself
Examining a Desire
Seeing the Whole Picture

The initial experiences obviously lend themselves best to narrative and descriptive writing—observing the world and recording those observations. But as the sequence proceeds, students begin to look for intangibles such as human relationships, personal desires, emotional attitudes. Here, it seems to us, Morgan makes a great leap—successfully—in composition teaching. As he approaches more and more abstract kinds of writing, he remains true to his central commitment to perception. As he says in the Preface, "Generalization is encouraged only insofar as it can be soundly based on sensory data." In effect, Morgan covers the ground of the expository rhetorical approach through the students' own eyes, without relying on rules and formulas. In fact, in using this approach ourselves, we have discovered that the formulas or patterns emerge in students' writing as a result of their improved perception; that is, as students become better and better at observing, they also become better at structuring their observations in writing. In a sense, the world and the student's observations of it take over the task traditionally given to the rules of expository rhetoric.

Several points of Morgan's teaching methods also deserve discussion. The title of the book comes from his technique of "here and now" writing, in which the students spend a sustained period of time, perhaps twenty minutes or more, writing down their perceptions, each sentence beginning with the phrase, *"Here and now. . . ."* This technique is rather like the freewriting of Peter Elbow (1973), though Morgan uses it principally as a means of marshalling thoughts rather than as a device for generating a wordy first draft.

Morgan also provides solid suggestions for gathering perceptions. In each chapter, he provides a poem, an excerpt from fiction, and a work of art for discussion. For example, in "Identifying with a Person," he provides a segment from James Baldwin's "Sonny's Blues" dealing with emerging personal relationships; Edward Arlington Robinson's poem, "Mr. Flood's Party," about a lonely elderly man; Jean François Millet's painting of a "Peasant Resting"; and a cartoon showing an ordinary citizen identifying with a statue of "the unknown citizen" (drawn from Auden's poem). In contrast to the literary models approach, Morgan does not ask students to imitate or critique the literature or art; rather, he has students describe their own perceptions on similar topics. The art and literature are used as a springboard into writing, an extremely fruitful technique that we will discuss as part of the *literary thematic* approach.

We find only two drawbacks to the perceptual approach practiced by Morgan. Unfortunately, he brings in traditional rhetorical categories from time to time and attempts to link them with perception. Thus he presents the old chestnut "comparison and contrast," then asks the students to perceive comparisons in the literature and art. We believe that those processes of perception are learned quite naturally and that Morgan runs the risk of limiting students' perceptions, not broadening them.

Perhaps more fundamental is the objection that by focusing exclusively on perception, the teacher may fail to do enough with helping students synthesize their ideas and get them down on paper. One can teach "seeing" at length without ever moving toward better writing. That weakness, we think, is remedied by the *experiential approach*, which we will now describe.

THE EXPERIENTIAL APPROACH. This method takes as its central premise that all good writing reflects a synthesis of experience; in other words, that we write best about what we know. But knowledge in this case does not simply mean facts or book learning; it represents a careful creation, in language, of what we perceive and how we relate those perceptions to past experience. Thus the experiential method subsumes many concerns of the percepual approach, but moves beyond it by making provision for the ways in which perceptions—experiences—are combined and processed by the writer and how they are worked out in writing. To draw on the current cliché, the experiential approach is committed to the belief that "writing is a way of knowing."

Further, at least as we practice it, this method holds to the philosophy that the basic skills and organizational structures of writing can be learned as one puts experience into words. It is the structure of experience, not rules of grammar or rhetoric, that shape words on a page. The experiential approach by no means ignores "the basics"; it incorporates them naturalistically, creating a flow of writing assignments that provides for increasing students' range of skills even as they extend their ability to write about diverse experiences in diverse ways.

There is no single pattern or model for an experience-based course (just as there is no rigid model for the other two approaches we have described in this section). Writing activities should be designed to meet the needs of the students coming into particular classes. At the same time, we find a general pattern emerging in the courses we have created at many different levels. In some respects, this pattern is similar to the simple-to-do complex structure of Morgan's perceptual approach. However, the experiential method incorporates a broader range of considerations—not just perception, but audience and author's role as well. The sequence moves:

From	To
Simple perceptions of the immediate, concrete world	Complex observations of events and issues
Basic reporting of observations	Evaluation and judging of ideas
Writing that is personal and private	Writing intended for increasingly broad audiences

From	To
Writing that comes from experiences already in the writer's head	Writing about new or fresh experience and knowledge

Often our courses can be broken into five stages or phases, with appropriate activities in each. (Chapter 3 on composition topics roughly follows those phases, so the reader can fill in the outline provided here with specific writing activities.)

1. *Introductions.* We lead off our courses spending considerable time having students get to know one another and the teacher. We introduce interest and experience inventories that encourage the students to get down on paper, usually in short phrases, some of the basic materials they have to work with as writers. The inventories then serve as a source of writing ideas for the early part of the course. In this respect our course is similar to Joseph Moore's, where students brainstorm for writing topics. Later we move the students toward acquiring and commenting on fresh experiences. At this introductory phase we describe the writing process as we perceive it and encourage the students to think about the various stages of writing as they have experienced them. We make clear our own experiential philosophy of writing so the students will understand why we are proceeding as we do.

2. *Exploring the Self Through Writing.* Every student we've ever met has dozens, if not hundreds, of good writing ideas inside his or her head just waiting to get out. Yet if you ask students to write, they claim they have nothing to say. We want students to discover that storehouse and to learn to get past experiences and personal ideas and thoughts down on paper. We introduce the idea of freewriting for those students who find it useful and suggest various free association techniques for evoking the flow. Topics for writing can be distant or recent memories, current personal concerns and problems, observations about past and present events. Often this writing is intense and personal, and the students may be reluctant to share it with others. We do not "push" for public readings; instead, we want students to gain strength and confidence writing from their own experience. We use journal writing at this phase, both to emphasize the private nature of writing and to encourage students to increase their fluency.

3. *Oneself and Others.* Moffett (1968) has written of the decreasing egocentricity of student writers as they mature. The older students become, the more they are able to move outside their immediate concerns to consider those of other people. We find that cycle is also repeated in experience-based writing courses. Once students have security to write about themselves, in private, they can begin to write about other people and to share their writing with audiences. Thus we offer writing activities that deal with people and human relationships, having students observe and describe those who make up their world. The writing workshop is introduced at this point, and we

begin to have students read their writing to one another, working in pairs, threes, and eventually small groups. We also encourage them to stretch out in the kinds of discourse forms they choose, urging them to write poems as well as personal essays or to explore their ideas on human relationships through fiction as well as first person narratives.

4. *Exploring the World.* Here the movement is toward gaining fresh knowledge, toward seeing what one has missed as well as discovering new knowledge and values. The students take up issues, problems, moral concerns. Many of the topics are those emphasized in an expository rhetoric course; however, we keep stressing the role that the writer, the self, plays in synthesizing and structuring ideas. In the writing workshop, the students generally become more and more skilled at serving as one another's editors, and frequently any discussions of content and structure originate with the students themselves rather than with the teacher.

5. *Investigating/Probing/Researching.* In this final phase the emphasis shifts from simple observation and evaluation—"opinion writing" as some call it—to more formal methods of acquiring and writing about knowledge. We do not teach "the research paper," but we help students learn a good many research skills. Often this part of the course is interdisciplinary, with students looking into issues and topics in subject areas that interest them. But we keep the writer and his or her perceptions at the heart of the writing process. Whether students are writing science papers or launching an investigation of an historical issue, we emphasize that the process is the same as it was when they wrote reminiscences and memoirs at the beginning of the course: The writer observes his or her world, thinks about it, makes observations, struggles to get those observations down on paper, and then anxiously awaits the response of readers.

(Note: A syllabus for one of our experience-based courses is provided in Appendix A.)

THE LITERARY-THEMATIC APPROACH. At the college level, discussion of literature in composition courses is likely to lead to hot debate. As we have suggested, many colleges have actually banned literature from writing courses because it tends to take over the course. Some people object, further, that literature should be studied as an end in itself, not "used" as a means of evoking writing from students.

We think it is very important to include literature in writing courses. In fact, we regret that in most curricula English faculties feel it necessary to put writing into separate courses. In an ideal world—or just a better one—English courses that naturally integrated reading and writing would exist so that literary study naturally led to written responses, and students' writing was treated as a kind of literature, worthy of serious reading and response in its own right.

Of course, literature can be abused in writing courses. It is an abuse of literature to treat it as a model for students to imitate. It is an abuse of literature to use it exclusively as a starting point for critical essays (college level) or book reports (the schools). It is an abuse of literature to use it as a "shocker" to elicit compositions, or, as some teachers do, to cut off reading in the middle and have students write their own endings, later to be compared to the author's.

We find that the solution to the question "What do we do with literature in the writing class?" can be found through the *transactional* theory of criticism and pedagogy of Louise Rosenblatt (1938, 1979). She states that reading a book involves a *transaction* between the reader and author: The reader responds to what the author has written on the page and creates meaning based on his or her own past experiences, perceptions, and values. In a very real sense, this transaction resembles the making of a composition, with the book, rather than real life, providing the raw materials of experience. It seems to us very natural to have students respond to literature in writing as they attempt to make sense of a text.

However, this does not mean having students write long interpretations or explications of the text. Instead, it involves having the students describe how the book touches them personally, telling how and why they respond to it as they do. The most common question we ask following the reading of literature is "Has anything like this ever happened to you?" Often those responses can be written, not just in essay form, but in any mode of discourse.

Nor does this seem to us to be an abuse of literature, for, as Rosenblatt says, the test of an author's skill is whether he or she makes contact with us as readers. The nature and depth of a reader's response is a test of the writer's success.

Having previously tried to discredit the literary models approach with its emphasis on imitation, we now want to modify that stand to suggest that bringing literature into the classroom provides examples that can, in fact, be useful to the student writer. But we are not advocating imitation. We simply think that having lots of good literature available in a writing course is bound to have a positive impact on students. Many professional writers make it clear that they attribute some of their success to the fact that they are voracious readers. As one reads, one absorbs ideas, techniques, strategies that later emerge, possibly unconsiously, in writing. We advocate literary immersion without slavish imitation.

The best method we know of immersing students in literature and encouraging them to write as well is the literary thematic approach. The teacher (possibly in consultation with students) chooses a topic or theme of interest to the group. It might deal with emotions (Love, Loneliness), ideas (Peace, Freedom), issues (Individual Rights, Mind Control), problems (Urban

Decay, The Quality of Leadership), or interdisciplinary studies (Ecology, Scientific Morality). The teacher collects many readings on the theme, fiction as well as nonfiction, poetry and drama as well as prose. In the literature "lessons," students examine both the literature itself and the themes that emerge, improving their ability as "transactionalists" in the process. Writing topics grow naturally from the students' responses to what they read, and students can compose papers ranging from private or personal statements to carefully researched position papers.

The literary thematic approach to reading and writing is not in wide use, and it is difficult to find good representative texts and syllabi. One of the best examples is the *Scholastic American Literature Program* (1977), prepared for use in high school courses. Although American literature is often taught as a chronological survey, Michael Spring, the Project Editor, chose to divide his literary selections into four thematic volumes, each with three subtopics:

WHO WE ARE
> *The Young*
> *The Old*
> *Men and Women*

WHERE WE LIVE
> *City and Country*
> *Journeys*
> *A Sense of Place*

HOW WE LIVE
> *At Work*
> *At Play*
> *At War*

WHAT WE BELIEVE
> *Personal Values*
> *American Myths and Dreams*
> *Fantasy and Imagination*

One could, of course, subdivide American literature into an infinite number of thematic units. The sixteen topics listed here seem to have broad appeal to high-school-age youngsters and to allow for a variety of topical discussions. Further, as the reader of this book may have noted, the "flow" of the topics from the self ("Who We Are") to issues and problems ("What We Believe") is similar to the structure we use in our own experience-based composition course.

Michael Spring invited one of us to work with his basic thematic selections and to develop writing topics so that the program could incorporate composition as well as literature. Given those themes, it was a relatively easy matter to create "transactional" topics such as the following:

For *Who We Are:*
Go back to your junior high or elementary school or to a neighborhood where you used to live. Have your memories 'drifted' with time? Write two sketches: the place as it is, and the place as you remembered it.

For *Where We Live:*
What have been some of the most important journeys in your life? Select one and write about it in detail. (Remember that a journey does not have to be a literal trip from one geographical place to another. You might want to write about a 'spiritual journey' in which you 'traveled' within your mind.)

For *How We Live:*
For many years in this country, the traditional family consisted of the male as 'breadwinner' and the female as 'homemaker.' Through reading and through interviewing members of your community, research the ways in which this traditional pattern is changing.

For *What We Believe:*
A utopia is a vision of an ideal world. As a class project, describe a utopia set in the year 3000. Working individually or in teams, describe such aspects of society as:

> the use and distribution of land
> politics
> war
> economy and finance
> family life
> social life
> transportation
> architecture

Such topics, four of perhaps eighty in the four volumes, draw indirectly on the students' reading, yet do not call for either imitation or literary analysis. We think they suggest the rich range of possible writing activities that can grow from a cautious use of literature in a literary thematic approach to composition.

Further, we think the approach ought to suggest to literature teachers ways of including writing in their courses. The transactional view of criticism makes it plain that the reader's personal response is important any time something is read. Students need not always write papers *about* literature in the literature class. They need not write just another set of papers analyzing form or theme or structure of character. They can describe their own transactions with literature. In our experience, having students write from literature in these ways enriches the class and does not distract or detract from it.

THE REAL WORLD TOPICS APPROACH. Similar in method to the literary thematic model, the topics approach looks to issues and problems outside the classroom and encourages students to develop their own reading and writing assignments, often with real audiences in mind.

The teacher and/or the students select an issue or problem—The Effects of Television, Energy, Controlling Technology, The Law and Human Rights, City Life, Work, Drug Abuse. Drawing on a classroom library prepared by the teacher or doing library research of their own, the students read in selected interest areas. Then they consider ways of using the written word to share their ideas with others.

In *Reality-Centered Learning*, Hy Ruchlis and Belle Sharefkin (1975) have students select topics from an inviting list that ranges from Education to World Law and then explore the resources that are available on that topic. The students become involved in learning how to structure their own learning (learning how to learn), and the topics have real and intrinsic value of their own. We think that Ruchlis and Sharefkin do not fully value reading and writing in their book, ignoring some good possibilities for literacy instruction, but, on the whole, their guide is extremely valuable for composition teachers.

CONFERENCING METHODS. The health spa where one of us exercises on rare occasions presents an interesting model of "instruction." The spa is essentially a gym, filled with weight lifting equipment, and is attractively carpeted, with music piped in. It is staffed by five people, all masters of the art of bodybuilding, who, on a busy day, will process between five and eight hundred people through the spa. (And we think *English* teachers have high class loads.) There is no real compulsion attached to the workout a member does at the spa. One consults with an instructor regularly to establish a program; the instructors are available to provide assistance as needed; but the individual member is responsible for monitoring his or her own progress.

Now it is dangerous to make comparisons between a composition course and a health spa, but it has always seemed to us that the spa provides a useful model for writing teachers. In effect, the spa instructors have learned how to individualize instruction on a large scale, so they can cope with a great many students, but deal with them on a one-to-one basis.

Conferencing methods in the writing course attempt to achieve the same thing. They break down the concepts of "class" and "lesson" and substitute face-to-face, instructor-to-student discussion of individual papers. Thomas Carnicelli (1980) of the University of New Hampshire reports that he literally does not meet his college writing courses as classes; instead, each student comes into his office once each week for a fifteen to twenty minute conference. Carnicelli has trained himself to read and respond to student writing on the spot, and he claims that even short conferences are more effective than whole class teaching. He further feels that conferencing this way promotes individual and independent learning.

Another "class-less" variation on conferencing is the writing laboratory approach being tried across the country. An exemplary lab is run by Mary Croft at the University of Wisconsin, Stevens Point. Her lab is a converted classroom, pleasantly decorated with art and samples of student writing, and includes a large reference shelf. Students who visit the lab are told that it is:

Not a proofreading, rewriting, correcting service.

Not a "we write it for you" service.

Not a grading service.

Not a guarantee of better grades.

It *is* a place where they can get specific help with specific writing problems (rather like the spa, where one can get individualized help depending on whether one wants to work on arms, shoulders, back, or tummy). Tutors, many of whom are prospective English teachers, work with students on a one-to-one basis. Sometimes students come in for regular appointments, but the lab is also available on a drop-in basis. What impressed us most in our visit to the Stevens Point lab is that it focuses on helping students with papers *in process*, instead of sentencing them to remedial drill or exercises.

However, despite the values of individualized conferencing, we're not altogether prepared to abandon the writing class. In the first place, it's not practical for most teachers. Few can, like Carnicelli, substitute office visits for regular class hours; in the schools that would be forbidden, and in college, where instructors often have to teach multiple sections of writing, it would lead to seven-day-a-week morn-'til-night office hours. Further, we also value the community aspect of the writing class. Even at the health spa where the bodybuilders are pursuing their own individualized programs there is camaraderie and sharing of goals and progress among the "regulars." In writing classes there is a need not only for peer group interchange, but for a sharing of successes.

The writing laboratory at Queens College, directed by Betsy Kaufman, is similar to the Stevens Point lab in providing on-the-spot help with papers in progress. But it also differs in working through group conferences. The students in the program meet in clusters each week to talk over their writing with one another and with a tutor. Thus they receive close, individualized attention but also have interaction with fellow student writers.

Still, a laboratory situation with a supply of writing tutors is a far cry from the situation of the typical school or college instructor, who may face ninety to 150 students anywhere from three to five times a week. Can conferencing work in those situations? We believe that it can and use in-class conferencing regularly in our own teaching.

Many variations are possible. Peter Elbow (1973), to whom we have referred frequently in this book, has worked toward perfecting a "teacherless" approach that is, in effect, a small group/conferencing method. Everyone in the group—teacher and students—writes regularly, and classes consist of sharing and reacting to papers. Elbow prefers to work with small groups of ten to fifteen, but much larger circles are possible. (The writing week of Joseph Moore, described elsewhere in this chapter, involves a large class circle at one point in the editorial process.)

In our own teaching, we have experimented with a variety of patterns. We prefer to have students work in editorial groups of two people during the early phases of a course. The teacher then circulates from pair to pair conducting "mini-conferences" of just a minute or two. Later, as the students gain confidence in themselves and their writing and as their writing nears an audience-ready stage, we place them in larger groups, perhaps four, five, or six. The teacher again drifts from group to group, joining in the conversation. Since it is difficult for the teacher to make contact with every student individually in these larger groups, we also provide "quiet" or workshop time in which the students work on drafts and revisions alone while the instructor confers with them privately. Finally, when egos are secure and papers completed, we hold whole class readings in which the teacher, in effect, confers publicly with each student about his or her paper.

Obviously, the "secret" to our method is to combine the positive effects of small-group and peer editing with those of individualized student-teacher conferences. When the students are working with each other, the teacher is freed to meet with students one to one. With that kind of arrangement it is not unrealistic to approach the sort of ideal of an instructor like Carnicelli, where individual guidance is frequent and systematic.

TOWARD A SYNTHESIS OF APPROACHES: THE POSSIBILITIES

Earlier in the chapter we commented on the dangers of trying to synthesize various approaches to writing, and we commented that many programs, courses, and textbooks seem to us a sad hodgepodge, a mindless mixing together of conflicting aims, values, and methods. At the same time, we fully recognize that a healthy synthesis of ideas is possible, that, given a coherent theory of teaching writing, an instructor might want to choose from among a variety of consistent approaches.

The six models we have presented here—*process, perception, experience, literary/thematic, real world topics,* and *conferencing*—have that kind of consistency and thus can be combined in many different ways. Though we profess that our courses fit the experiential model, we draw freely on the others: We include the major features of the process approach; we are concerned about improving perceptions; we use literature as a starting point for writing; we have our students write on real world topics; and we employ conferencing. We want to encourage readers of this book to experiment with similar mixes to find an approach that they find satisfactory.

In surveying composition course materials and descriptions, we found one course description that seemed to us an extremely good model of synthesis. It was sent to us by Anita Brostoff and Lois Josephs Fowler (1979) of Carnegie-Mellon University. They teach a professional writing course for non-English majors—students interested in engineering, science, business, and design—and thus their course had to serve a practical function. But Brostoff and Fowler also wanted to make it more than just an applied writing course; they wanted it to make "systematic use of basic research in composition."

In reviewing the research, they were impressed by the consistency of interest, first, in writing as process, and second, in the use of peer feedback. They also appear to have been influenced by the literature on experience-based approaches and chose a sequence of activities "moving from personal considerations to social concerns":

> There were four papers, each with a specific audience: (1) what constitutes professional success in your field?—audience, a future employer; (2) the media and your profession—audience, an administrator for a local television station, newspaper, radio station, or public relations firm; (3) ethical considerations in your profession—audience, a professional organization in your field; and (4) the relationship of any current issue to your profession—audience, the public.

A tidy sequence, we think. If the reader checks those four assignments against our six models in this chapter, he or she will find most of them represented here. Incorporated in the assignments were a sequence of conferences as well as guided individual reading.

Despite the fact that these assignments were not intended to be overtly "practical" (e.g., they did not instruct students in the specific techniques of engineering writing or business writing), the instructors nevertheless found that students were satisfied with the learning in this sequence:

> Having acquired improved writing skills, they recognized that they would be able to write memos and reports as well as articles, and they sometimes incorporated these forms within the context of an article. They used

rhetorical techniques, though we never openly presented them as models, to bring home what they had to say.

In other words, while holding consistent with contemporary research, Brostoff and Fowler also found that they had effectively covered the content expected in the traditional rhetorical expository or basic skills course.

Their model cannot be transferred directly into other teaching situations. One cannot and should try to duplicate their structure with other kinds of students. At the same time, their spirit of inquiry and discovery and their willingness to create a synthesis based on contemporary research very much deserves to be emulated.

CHAPTER 8

ASSESSMENT AND GRADING

The topic of this chapter, the assessment of writing (or, more broadly, the assessment of writing, writers, and writing programs), is complex and, for most teachers, frustrating. Much of the confusion can be traced to a single problem: defining "good" writing. Interpretations and values differ from one reader to another, from one situation to another, from one teacher to another, and what constitutes good writing for a readership one day may be very bad writing for another readership on a different day. Terms like "assessment" and "grading" imply a degree of scientific rigor and precision, yet evaluators of writing and writing programs often find themselves trying to walk on quicksand, where the surface looks solid, but is an illusion.

Over the years, many researchers have attempted to create solid ground in the bog of evaluation, developing tools and measures that give objectivity to writing assessment. Sometimes their discussion becomes stuck in a quagmire itself, as it did in an article we recently read where the researcher bandied about such terms as "situational specificity," "metacognitive response," "the hypothesis generating heuristic," "protocol verification," "the principles of complementarity and redundancy," and "the cohort confound."

We will not be drawn into marshlands of formal research here. Instead, we will describe procedures that will be helpful to the classroom teacher of writing, drawing on the research techniques where they are helpful, but for the most part focusing on assessment methods which, while possibly less rigorous than those used in formal experiments, yield interesting, useful results.

It is important at the outset to make clear the distinction between two words in the chapter title: "assessment"[1] and "grading." For many teachers, the two are synonymous, for in the end all the assessment they do boils down to a single grade entered on a report card or transcript. Many of the

---

[1] We also want to make clear that in discussing assessment in this chapter, we have in mind evaluation of the growth of individual writers and the collective growth of groups of writers—individual classrooms and whole schools—rather than the evaluation and subsequent revision of individual papers, discussed at length in Chapter 5.

discussions on these twin topics have themselves been reduced to a single question, "How can I derive a grade for the students in my writing courses?"

Although the grading question is a serious one—we struggle with it every term we teach—it is important for teachers not to see grading as the only kind of assessment that exists. Indeed, assessment is a very broad term, encompassing many kinds of evaluation processes and activities, while grading is much more specific and limited. Because of that, we will take up assessment first, describing the dimensions of strong evaluation programs for writing; then we will discuss the more specific—and in some ways, more complex—problem of grading.

WHY ASSESS WRITING AND WRITING PROGRAMS?

Why indeed? If assessing writing is so complex, why bother with it at all? Why seek points of agreement where none exist? Why try to achieve objectivity and precision if writing itself is subjective and, in its way, imprecise? Why venture into the swamp when we can see at a distance that it is wet and muddy? We can think of five good reasons for developing a solid assessment program despite the obvious difficulties and the treacherous footing:

1. *A good assessment program can help students learn better.* In a sense, this is the only reason one needs to justify assessment, for if it is right—if assessment *does* help students learn to write better—it belongs in the program. The formal research on evaluation of writing is shaky in describing the relationship between evaluation and writing skill. Still, it is apparent that evaluation is an intrinsic part of the writing process itself—every writer either seeks or is subject to evaluation of his or her work. We're convinced that evaluation can and does make a difference, provided that it is directed to students and their needs, not simply to the felt needs of teachers or administrators.

2. *Assessment can prove that teachers are doing their jobs.* This is a spurious reason, as far as we are concerned, but in the current climate in the schools and colleges, it is an important one. All over the country teachers are being asked to be "accountable" for their work, to show results for tuition or tax dollars spent. A good assessment program can produce the kinds of results parents and students want to see. At the same time, it is important to caution that an obsession with showing results can get totally out of control and possibly even destroy a program. (In many Federal programs, researchers must spend more money on evaluation than they do on instructional materials, an unfortunate state of affairs.)

3. *Assessment can help teachers improve courses and programs.* This might be labeled the "developmental" function of evaluation. Assessing what one does allows one to do it better. As a corollary, we can add: *Assess-*

ment can also help teachers improve their teaching. Without systematic evaluation, the changes that take place in courses, programs, and teaching styles are random and, frequently, pointless. A good program of evaluation should lead to improved teaching as well as to improved writing on the part of the students.

4. *Assessment can contribute to understanding the teaching/learning process.* There is much that is not known about how to teach writing. Professional meetings of writing teachers are anything but harmonious, and seldom are participants in full accord about what we ought to be doing in school and college courses. Whether or not one writes for publication or gives speeches at professional gatherings, a good evaluation program helps the individual teacher contribute to the common store of knowledge about writing. And, in a very real sense, every practicing teacher has an obligation to make whatever contributions he or she can. It may be tempting for teachers to wait for "research" to tell them how to proceed in their courses, but we feel that the most obvious progress in writing instruction takes place when teachers explore and experiment, evaluate what they are doing, and share those results with other teachers.

5. *Assessment leads to professional growth.* Schools and colleges that develop evaluation programs often find a fringe benefit: that the process is excellent in-service training. One cannot evaluate writing and writing programs without asking some fundamental questions: What are we doing? Why are we doing it? Does doing it this way make any sense? Are there better ways? Answering those questions—or, more accurately, seeking answers to them—can lead to changes in faculty beliefs and attitudes that can affect the entire curriculum.

There is a sixth reason for assessing, one that we will discuss in more detail later. Like evaluating to prove to your superiors that you are doing something, this reason is spurious to the educational process itself; yet in the practical world of teaching, it is very important:

6. *Assessment can lead to sound ways of giving grades.*

WHAT TO EVALUATE?

WRITING.   The most obvious answer to that question—writing—may also be simplistic. Of course, looking at students' papers to see how well or badly they write is an important part of the assessment program. No multiple choice or fill-in-the-blank test will suffice to tell whether students have mastered writing skills, and there seems to be no tests-and-measurements substitute for analyzing actual samples of student writing.

At the same time, given the fact that the values and tastes of readers differ, evaluating writing is not as simple as it seems. In many cases, discussion of the quality of a paper can lead to violent disagreements in faculty meetings, with people perceiving a single paper as being everything from "awful" to "remarkable." Most research indicates that without careful training and prior agreement on standards, readers' opinions about writing quality vary so widely as to be almost useless. There are some ways of refining these kinds of judgments, and we will suggest ways of approaching the assessment of writing samples further on in the chapter.

Further, actual writing—the product—may not be the only valid measure of whether a student or a writing program is succeeding. For one thing, some students may come into a course writing reasonably well, so their achievements may not be solely attributable to instruction (a question that can only be answered with the use of carefully controlled pre- and post-test measures). For another, students' performances on writing samples may not be indicative of their overall ability. A writing sample—particularly if carefully controlled—may seem like a test and thus induce poor or atypical writing. On the other hand, a writing sample elicited within the friendly confines of a writing course may bear no relationship at all to the student's performance outside in "the real world."

It is important to look at writing, and some sort of writing sample should, in our judgment, be at the heart of an assessment program. But the sample should be read and evaluated with great caution, and it should be only one of several different areas of measurement.

STUDENT SKILLS AND ATTITUDES. Throughout this book we have advocated a process approach to composition, one that teaches activities and skills rather than the structure or content of completed pieces of discourse. Consequently, we think evaluation of the writing *process* is important. Have students mastered such basic skills as gathering information, assessing the needs of an audience, editing their work critically, proofreading and copyediting papers into a form acceptable to an audience? Examining students' attitudes toward writing may also be a legitimate measure of the success of a course. Do the students like to write (or, at least, do they not actively despise it)? Do they feel confident of their ability to confront new writing tasks and situations successfully? Do they care about reaching audiences; do they respect the audiences for which they write?

Assessing these kinds of skills and attitudes is even more difficult than looking at actual writing samples—a writing sample, at least, holds still while one looks at it. Even so, there are many ways one can discover whether the processes have been mastered, ranging from simple direct observation to collecting notes, diaries, and rough drafts. Attitudes can be assessed through questionnaires as well as through observation and student diaries.

TEACHERS' SKILLS. To some extent, the teacher's successes are indicated by the writing students produce, but again the measure is only indirect. While the production of good writing is one important aim, the teacher may have many other goals for the class, among them fostering interaction in peer groups, teaching students to be independent critics of their own work, and providing the class with a wide range of audiences for publication of writing. Sometimes the teacher's self-evaluation can consist of a simple checklist: "Yes, I did provide opportunities for publication outside of class." "No, I didn't get every student to master copyediting skills." At other times, student questionnaires may provide answers, and formal course evaluations serve as an obvious and useful route to teacher evaluation. Occasionally, the evaluation may be done by outsiders: by a department head or a school or college administrators. It can even be done through electronic media, with classes videotaped for review by either the teacher or his or her superiors.

COURSE OR PROGRAM GOALS. "I planned my course meticulously," teachers have been known to say, "and at the beginning of the term, the wrong students came in the door." A writing course is presumably designed to meet the needs of individual students, but due to the nature of the academic system, much of the planning must be done before the students arrive. Thus teachers find themselves committed more or less firmly to a syllabus or locked into a composition textbook or rhetorical reader for a term. Usually, teachers attempt to solve this problem by aiming at a middle ground—the hypothetical average student—and slanting course goals toward him or her. And then, of course, that average student—the one for whom the course would be perfect—never shows up.

It is important for the instructor to develop evaluation measures to determine whether or not course goals meet the needs of the real students who arrive the first day of class and who remain for the term. Evaluation can begin on that first day, continue while the class is in progress, and follow through in a final course evaluation. Are the course aims valid? Did the course teach what the students expected it would? Did it meet what the students perceive to be their needs? Are there other goals that should be included in future offerings of the course?

Collection of reliable data in this area is extremely difficult. Students are not always the best judges of their own needs (not that teachers are necessarily any better). No composition course we've taught has ever satisfied all the students, and there are always other activities and goals that our students tell us we should have included. If one took *all* the advice students have to offer about goals, courses would become too elaborate to teach. At the same time, there is often a pattern to students reponses which, studied carefully and critically, can help the instructor change the direction of a course to suit the needs of a greater number of students.

COURSE ACTIVITIES.   The heart of the course is the activities in it. What do the students do? Do they write? Talk? Read and discuss literature? Work in small groups? Revise? Proofread? The course activities allow the instructor to move from a fairly abstract set of goals toward improved student performance. We think it is important to build in formal or informal evaluation of every activity—every lesson—in a course. Sometimes the evaluation can be based on simple observation: "Yes, the students did, in fact, spend the hour critiquing one another's work." At other times it can involve systematic inspection of a set of papers looking for a particular trait, say, the use of concrete detail or the awareness of an audience. Student feedback forms may provide assistance, as may the remarks of an external observer who comments on whether or not an activity seemed successful. Perhaps more than any other form of evaluation, a review of course activities can supply the instructor with a sense of the value of many aspects of the course: the goals and objectives, his or her own skills, the quality of writing being produced. Evaluation of activities can thus serve as a kind of umbrella under which a wide range of course components and student behaviors come into critical review.

A SAMPLER OF ASSESSMENT TECHNIQUES

We are suggesting, in essence, that assessment of a writing program should take place at many points, not just at the end. It should focus not only on writing, but on the teaching and learning skills and processes that make up the course. It should be an integral part of the course.

"But," many instructors may object, "all that takes time. Thorough assessment could become so time consuming that there is no time for anything else."

We grant that as a legitimate concern, and certainly we do not want to see evaluation become an end in itself.[2] A solution to that problem, we think, lies in a distinction between formal educational research (the sort written up in the educational journals) and what we will label *practical classroom evaluation*. In formal research, the investigator must be extremely careful that individual evaluation techniques do not somehow influence or skew performance (just as a scientist makes certain that a thermometer he or she is

[2] In many public schools assessment already has become an end in itself. At local levels, administrators have substituted massive testing programs for actual program development. A great many state departments of education have launched assessment programs—usually multiple choice tests of writing—that consume millions of taxpayer dollars without providing useful results for classroom teachers. We can only lament this misuse of tests, which is often political rather than pedagogical in nature, and offer the argument that the kind of assessment program we describe here can not only satisfy the felt needs of administrators and the general public, but can be useful to teachers and students as well.

about to insert into a liquid is already at or near the temperature of the liquid). Students of educational psychology know of the "Hawthorne effect," in which members of an experimental group perform better than they would ordinarily because they know they are part of a "special" group.

While the researcher must guard against such "contamination," the classroom teacher need not particularly fear it. Of course, one does not want to bias results to the point where they are completely inaccurate, but the classroom teacher is interested principally in achieving results with students, not with statistical or methodological purity.

This belief, in turn, leads us to suggest the principle that *classroom evaluation measures should contribute directly to instruction.* That is, the evaluation program one develops ought not only to yield data of interest to the evaluator, it ought to be directly useful in the classroom. For example, we favor the use of student self-assessment measures over standardized tests, for the former give writers direct help in writing better, while the latter yield information that is principally useful to outsiders: teachers, administrators, parents. Similarly, if we take a writing sample, we are more concerned that it represent a student's best writing than that it be gathered under tightly controlled, replicable conditions.

The following assessment techniques seem to us to have practical use in the classroom in addition to providing useful data. In constructing an evaluation program, we suggest that the instructor review these techniques (and others that can be found in the professional literature) and choose those that will satisfy the twin aims of providing useful assessment information while improving the quality of the instruction.

EVALUATING WRITTEN PIECES. We have already discussed our belief that assessing writing on the basis of a standardized test that does not actually examine writing is invalid. Despite the persistence and popularity of these tests, particularly when large numbers of students must be examined, there is no evidence in the professional literature to show a high degree of correlation between success at answering short answer or multiple choice items and the ability to write. (For a detailed discussion of the flaws of one widely used, nonwritten test of verbal ability, the Scholastic Aptitude Test, see Nairn and Nader, 1980.)

If we want to see how well students write, we must examine some of their writing. And there is no getting away from the fact that collecting writing samples is time consuming and (if one is conducting a mass testing program) expensive. The simplest and most practical sample the classroom teacher can take is the *writing portfolio,* a file folder containing the work students have prepared during a term. As believers in learning to write through experience, we think an informal assessment of the portfolio can tell volumes about a student's skills, and in a great many school and college settings the portfolio is sufficient to provide evidence that the student (and the teacher) is performing. If the portfolio is filled with a variety of kinds of discourse after a term or half term, there is at least some reason to believe that writing is being taught. If it contains just a few scraps of paper, one has to question whether a program is truly concerned with developing writing skills.

But other, more systematic methods of assessment are possible. The simplest is an *objectives checklist,* in which the teacher makes a list of the fundamental goals of the writing course and determines by examining the portfolio whether they have been achieved. Thus if writing papers in a variety of modes is an aim, the teacher can determine whether the student has written different kinds of papers (the teacher, of course, has defined what he or she means by "variety" in advance). If the teacher is concerned with developing research skills or creative writing abilities or consciousness of an audience, he or she can see those reflected in the portfolio. Often this kind of assessment can be done through *conferencing,* in which the student and teacher sit down to review the portfolio and the course objectives together. Such face-to-face discussion is precisely the kind of in-process evaluation we think is valuable because it provides help to the student while giving evaluation data to the teacher.

Pure researchers, of course, would be unhappy with something as informal as a writing portfolio. "Too many variables are uncontrolled," they might say. "We don't know how long the students spent on their various writings; they didn't write on the same topics to make comparison possible; the teacher may have provided more help for some students than for others." Although we are generally satisfied with the results of assessing portfolios, we recognize that many schools and colleges are concerned with taking a sample the pure researcher would call "reliable." In that way, administrators can examine the effectiveness of a writing program for an entire school or district as well as coming up with data that show how individual students are performing relative to other members of their peer group.

The writing for these samples must be controlled rather closely. Students must write on the same topic (or on very similar topics) pre- and post-test, with identical instructions and under common constraints of time. Unfortunately, these controls often have the effect of forcing the student to write badly. What if the student doesn't like the topic or have anything to say about it? He or she must write anyway. What if the writer has more to say than the time allows? Too bad; cut it short. Aware of these problems, researchers have made some attempts to "humanize" these kinds of writing tests. In the National Assessment of Educational Progress (about the only national examination that works principally with actual writing samples), topics are designed to be as creative and engaging as possible. Students may be given several different ways to complete a task, and imaginary audiences are built in to provide focus for papers. The NAEP even encourages students to jot down notes and to prepare a revised final draft. Still, a test is a test, and any common sampling situation is likely to have overtones of testing that may lead to students' writing atypically. In the end, composition faculties need to decide whether the precision and reliability gained through common sampling outweighs the problems induced by the sampling procedure. (For a discussion of the problems encountered by a large city school district in conducting a sample of writing, see Suhor, *Mass Testing in Composition: Is It Worth Doing Badly?*, 1977.)

Whether one chooses to do rigorous or informal sampling, we think the teacher/reader needs to follow consistent procedures in the evaluation of students' papers. Individual judges of writing are notoriously biased, particularly if the students happen to be their *own*, so it may be useful to introduce various kinds of scales and guides for evaluation, and, quite possibly, to involve outsiders or second readers in the process. This complicates the scoring but also makes it more dependable.

A commonly used evaluation scheme—one, in fact, that seems to have taken the country by storm—is a *"holistic"*[3] approach developed by Diederich (1974). It involves the entire English faculty (as well as other interested faculty) in evaluating two samples of student writing, pre- and post-test. Two readers read each paper, examining such characteristics as *ideas, organization, wording, flavor, usage, punctuation, spelling,* and *handwriting.* After some training, most readers can find a high degree of agreement in ranking such traits holistically on a scale of 2 (low) to 10 (high). If they disagree on the ranking of an individual paper, a third reader is brought in to resolve the differences. Teachers who have been through the process say that it works well and that it provides a useful fringe benefit: It forces faculty members to talk to one another about writing. At the same time, they report, the Diederich method involves a great deal of planning and staff time, and, because of the impressionism involved, the results it provides are at best vague.

---

[3] The term "holistic" is much bandied about and deserves some discussion and definition. Cooper describes holistic evaluation as a "guided procedure for sorting or ranking written pieces" (Cooper and Odell, 1977, p. 3). He shows that it can involve anything from impressionistic sorting to careful analysis of writing traits as in the Diederich scheme. Frequently, one sees the word spelled in the professional literature as "wholistic," a legitimate variant, which emphasizes that the procedure involves the rating of compositions in their entirety, rather than looking at fragmentary skills or traits. The term itself has its origins in the philosophical system of holism, which held that the whole is greater than the sum of the parts. Ironically, the Diederich method, and a great many of the holistic rating schemes we have examined, conflicts with that philosophy by attempting to measure the whole by assessing its individual parts or components, even though the parts are judged holistically. "Holistic" is thus another of those boggy terms.

Another evaluation method that is increasingly used in schools and colleges is *primary trait scoring* (which may, or may not, be a "holistic" method). Under this procedure, individual teachers or the faculty as a whole describe, in detail and possibly with supporting sample papers, the traits or features that ought to appear in students' writing if the instructional program is working. Fairly abstract features can be evaluated by this technique, including such matters as *point of view, imaginativeness, consciousness of audience, personal voice,* and *narrative flow.* The raters make broad judgments in three categories: *Yes,* the paper or passage contains this trait; *No,* it doesn't; or, *Not Enough Evidence to Judge.* The usefulness of primary trait scoring is that the information it provides is quite specific. Further, because of its Yes-No, forced decision procedure, it avoids some of the haziness of a rating scale such as Diederich's.

The possibilities for formal evaluation of papers are almost endless. They range from extremely reliable (but instructionally unhelpful) *counting procedures,* where the evaluator counts observable features—errors, number of words, T-units—to informal methods such as Stake's *responsive evaluation* (Snow, 1979), in which readers simply describe what they see happening and then evaluate it according to criteria that they state clearly and plainly. Obviously, any school or college faculty interested in a mass testing program would want to review all of these possibilities before selecting a commercially published examination or, perhaps, developing its own test.

At the same time, we think individual teachers may want to consider the kind of precision that any of these techniques can add to their classroom evaluation of student writing. For example, Diederich's rating scales can easily be adapted for use in judging individual papers or writing portfolios. Primary trait scoring can help teachers describe exactly how students have or have not managed to get particular qualities into their writing. Responsive evaluation represents a solid refinement of the conventional subjective evaluation of student work. Thus whether or not one goes to a mass testing program with tight controls, the techniques described here and in the evaluation literature can considerably improve the assessment program.

SURVEYS, QUESTIONNAIRES, AND ATTITUDE SCALES.   Where evaluating a writing sample can be time consuming, this category of assessment yields quick results, though the data often reflects writing skills only indirectly. For example, as we suggested in Chapters 3 and 7, we like to begin our writing courses with a simple *writing inventory* to assess student interests and attitudes. We ask students to complete a questionnaire describing their "best" and "worst" writing assignments in previous schools or courses and what made those assignments seem bad or good. (Our interest is not in checking up on previous teachers, but on discovering what the students like to write about.) We have students describe the writing process as they practice it, and we ask them to tell us a little about the aspects of writing that give them difficulty. Such questionnaires can be given at any time during the writing course or program. They can be used to determine whether students feel they are making progress in the course, whether they feel they are learning to write better, whether they are frustrated by some tasks and assignments.

Most questionnaires are open-ended, which is to say they ask a question and leave a blank space for the respondent to fill in. The open-ended instrument encourages people to pour out their feelings, but it also makes it possible for them to hide or mask responses by making their answers vague or short. *Attitude scales* may be used, possibly in conjunction with an open-ended questionnaire, to solve this problem. McAndrew (1980) describes a scale to measure attitudes toward the arts that he uses at the beginning and end of an interdisciplinary humanities courses. He presents a series of descriptive statements—"I really enjoy listening to classical music"; "I would never read literature unless somebody made me"—and asks students to react on a scale of 1 ("strongly disagree") to 5 ("strongly agree"). This kind of scale, no doubt one familiar to the reader, can easily be adapted for questions about writing:

I'd rather write a letter than phone somebody long distance.
   1   2   3   4   5
Getting started is the most difficult part of writing.
   1   2   3   4   5
Writing short stories is more fun than writing essays.
   1   2   3   4   5

We have often adapted that kind of scale to help students evaluate specific course activities:

INSTRUCTIONS: Rate the value or usefulness of the following course assignments or activities on a scale of 1 ("not very useful, useless") to 5 ("extremely helpful or valuable"):

Writing a chapter of your autobiography.
   1   2   3   4   5
Researching a topic in a field that interests you.
   1   2   3   4   5
Evaluating and responding to other people's writing.
   1   2   3   4   5

With this kind of scale, we usually leave blank spaces following each item for comments. We find that often students want to amplify the opinions registered on the forced choice scale so that a combination of approaches yields more information than using either a questionnaire or a scale alone might.

There are so many different scales and other measuring devices that it is impossible to comment on all their applications and possibilities in writing programs. But the reader can speculate about the possible uses of such well-established measures as:

> *The semantic differential*—the respondent characterizes his or her attitudes using descriptive opposites: "strong/weak," "active/passive," "hot/cold."
>
> *Ranking scales*—activities or processes are listed in order of value or importance to the respondent, producing a list of "most valued" to "least valued."
>
> *Like me/not like me*—students are asked to describe whether statements accurately portray them; for example, "I like to write slowly, getting it down just right the first time."
>
> *Q-sort*—a series of statements or descriptions of processes must be divided into a predetermined number of categories, thus forcing the respondent to make value judgments.

Questionnaires and scales can also be useful to teachers in assessing their own performance. Rosen (1980) has developed a scale and checklist that teachers can use to sort through the kinds of comments they put on students' papers. By studying whether those comments are principally negative or positive, whether they are devoted to correction or editing, whether they are simple evaluative comments or include instructional suggestions, the teacher (or, perhaps, a supervisor) can determine whether evaluation procedures are consistent and in keeping with current research. Drawing on the work of Emig and Parker [1976], she also uses the results of this survey to help teachers understand *why* they grade the way they do—what in their background as writers, teachers, or students leads them to value particular kinds of comments.

Finally, simple checklists can serve as a useful form of assessment, reminding teachers of their basic aims and objectives and helping them determine whether they have done everything they set out to do. Here is such a checklist prepared by the Ontario Ministry of Education. Because it bears directly on writing instruction, we will reprint it *in toto*. (In this checklist, both "yes" and "no" may be "right" answers.)

Evaluation of Learning Environment

_____ Do students ever read in my subject area voluntarily?

_____ How many kinds of reading material do I make available?

_____ Can students with reading problems get information through other means (e.g., tapes of the text)?

_____ Do students know enough about the subject to comprehend what I ask them to read?

_____ Do students have time/opportunity to talk about what they have read?

_____ Do they have opportunity to do nonassigned writing on the subject?

_____ Do students ever write for me voluntarily?

_____ How frequently and how much do they write?

_____ Do I encourage writing?

_____ Is all written work marked? (Should it be?)

_____ Do my students always write for me as for "an examiner"?

_____ What range of writing functions is represented in my assignments?

_____ Do I permit and encourage "expressive" writing?

_____ Do I provide opportunity for poor writers to work up to "final draft" language gradually?

CONFERENCES.   Moving beyond "paper and pencil" means of assessment, we find conferences an extremely useful method of evaluation. At one end of a continuum is the _formal conference_ in which the teacher and an individual student meet, preferably in a place where their discussion can be private, to discuss individual papers and the student's growth in the course. At the college level, time for conferencing can often be found through the instructor's office hours, with students scheduled to come in once, twice, or several times during the term. Some college instructors will cancel formal classes for a week or so to create extra time for conferences. In the schools, where classes cannot be cancelled, where students must be met five days a week, and where office hours do not exist, finding the time for a conference is more difficult. One of the most satisfactory means we have explored is combining conferencing with free or guided reading periods so that most of the students are busy reading while the teacher conducts conferences of five to ten minutes with individual students.

Small group conferences also provide a solution to the problem of finding time, although they lack the intimacy and the individualized attention of the private conference. Still, many students share common writing problems, and given the importance of peer group discussion and feedback, a group conference guided by the teacher can be successful, not only for evaluating writing, but for helping students learn how to critique one another's work.

We are personally most comfortable with the _process conference_, less formal, which is conducted as a regular part of the writing workshop. The teacher simply makes it a point to visit with as many students as possible during class writing and revision periods, glancing at writing in progress, comparing it to work previously done, coaching the students in areas that need work. We find that these conferences—often *mini-conferences* of just a few seconds—can be conducted more frequently than formal conferences and that, in the end, they provide for a more sustained form of evaluation.

Whatever its form, the conference is important because it provides face-to-face evaluation. Charles Duke (1975) recommends that English teachers borrow from the techniques of client-centered counseling in the conference by:

Focusing on specific papers, specific problems.

Clarifying what he or she sees the student is trying to accomplish.

Using *acceptance and approval words* both for the work the student has done and his or her attempts to improve it.

Using *reassurance phrasing* to support the student's efforts.

Providing *nondirective leads* that help the students see alternative ways of achieving their aims and goals.

The goal of all of this, as Duke explains, is "to help the student reach the point where he feels comfortable talking about his writing and where he becomes willing to examine it on his own, inside and outside the conference environment."

JOURNALS, DIARIES, AND LOGS.   In describing *responsive evaluation* we emphasized the importance of description, of simply telling what is happening in a piece of writing prior to evaluating it. To this end, various kinds of recordkeeping devices can be used by both the teacher and the student to make notes, observations, and evaluative comments.

We have had our students keep a log called the *rhetoric of the imagination* (Miller and Judy, 1978). It is, in effect, a kind of *writer's notebook* for notes and drafts, ideas and jottings, even rough drafts. We also ask them to make a running commentary on their thoughts, concerns, and problems as they write, so the log becomes a detailed summary of the student's growth and development as a writer.

We also keep *teacher logs* ourselves, notebooks that contain jottings on whole classes as well as individual students. In monitoring activities we often jot down ideas about lessons in retrospect, analyzing what happened and how the lesson might have been done differently and more successfully. This is the place for notes on student conferences, notes taken either in the presence of the student or written down later. The purpose of the log is to collect and store data on what happens in a course for purposes of evaluation. As a final stage in evaluation, it may be useful for both the students and the teacher to bring their logs or diaries to class and to spend a class period reminiscing, going back to thoughts, feelings, and accomplishments throughout the course to sense the growth that has taken place.

CONSTRUCTING AN EVALUATION PROGRAM

We hope this sampler of assessment procedures has made it obvious that although the evaluation of writing, writers, and writing courses and programs is not easy, there are many ways one can go about it successfully. The problem is one of picking and choosing from among the various possibilities. An evaluation program should be solid without becoming so complex that it detracts from the course or the program itself.

One useful model for developing a program draws on an acronym used by Daniel Stufflebeam (Snow, 1979), CIPP: *Context, Input, Process,* and *Product*. A good evaluation program, he suggests, will sample at a variety of points in the program, using a variety of different kinds of evaluation measures. The *context* of the program is its setting and its students. The writing teacher would ask: Who am I teaching? Why? The teacher might use "homemade" inventories in conjunction with judicious scanning of test scores to get a fix on the students in the class. He or she might collect an initial writing sample to determine how well or badly they write and hold an informal class discussion in which the students talk about their personal interests and their feelings about a writing course. At the end of context evaluation, the teacher ought to feel he or she has a good sense of the students' needs.

Input evaluation centers on the instructional program itself: goals, materials, course activities. The teacher might decide to use student rating scales to evaluate the usefulness or appropriateness of course activities and draw on conferences as a means of determining how well things are going. An important part of this evaluation is to determine whether the "inputs" do, in fact, match the students' needs as previously determined in context evaluation.

Process evaluation obviously deals with course activities as well, this time focusing on what actually occurs within the classroom. Logs and diaries are one record of process; teacher observations are another; small group discussions are a third. At this phase, the teacher is concerned not so much with goals or outcomes but with the quality of experiences students are having in the class. Are they having an authentic experience with writing or does their work seem to them a dummy run? Are the small group discussions fruitful? When the students revise, do papers get better?

Finally, *product* evaluation is concerned with the quality of writing produced, and here the teacher might draw on a writing sample, on student portfolios, and on a range of evaluation techniques from impressionistic readings to rigorous scoring.

The CIPP model is only one way of looking at an evaluation program. It might be too elaborate for some schools, where a simple pre-test, post-test sampling might be judged more satisfactory. Or CIPP might seem too informal in a setting where rigorous accountability measures are in effect. However, we see it as an excellent starting point for an evaluation program. At the very least, it can suggest ways for writing instructors to develop methods of course evaluation that are genuinely useful to themselves and to their students.

GRADING

As a system of assessment, grading is highly unsatisfactory. The detrimental effects of grading on students' performance is well documented in the professional literature (Raths, Harmin, Simon 1972). Grades induce false levels of performance; they fail to communicate substantive information to the person whose work is being evaluated; they are highly subjective and statistically unreliable; they are used to pigeonhole and sort students into broad and unmerited categories; they blur the distinction between personal self-worth and actual performance.

In a composition course, grades can have an insidious effect, encouraging students to write for the grade and to emphasize pleasing the instructor instead of learning to write for personal satisfaction. In our chapter on revision we suggested that students ought to become more and more skilled at learning to edit their own work, but grading systems operate against that skill. We find in our own classes that placing letter grades on papers interferes with communicating openly and honestly with students about the qualities of their writing, for, in the end, all comments boil down to the evaluation contained in the grade.

In short, we see the grading system as one of the genuine evils of school and college writing programs. We find no redeeming values in grades, and if given a choice, we would not even consider using them as a method of evaluation in a writing program.

But in our teaching situation, we don't have a choice about whether or not to give grades, and neither, we suspect, do most of the readers of this book. Grades are a stock part of school and college educational programs. They are used by other schools and by employers to judge applications. Students, it is said, want to be graded on their work (a claim we doubt). Other instructors clearly want to have the power contained in grades to induce motivation in their students. The grading system, we fear, will be with us for a long time to come.

Consequently, the existence of grades presents a dilemma. We propose to solve it by placing the giving of grades within the broader context of assessment programs. (Our insistence on separating grading from assessment and discussing grading last is thus explained.) The negative effects of grading can be minimized if a strong assessment program is in operation. If a variety of pre- and post-instructional evaluation methods are in use, if students are receiving both process and product feedback, if an instructor is assessing student needs and determining whether or not instruction meets those needs, if students are strongly encouraged to engage in self-evaluation and self-assessment, then actual letter grades need not be overly destructive; in fact, they can serve as a crude, but accurate summary of a student's performance in a course.

The professional literature is filled with various schemes for arriving at grades. Some teachers set up elaborate point and counting schemes; some begin with a blanket grade, say "B," and let students work up or down; some grade separately for content and mechanics; others apply a single, "holistic" grade to a paper. We will not review the myriad systems that are possible. Rather, we will discuss four broad categories of grading plans that seem reasonably practical and, within the constraints imposed by grading systems themselves, accurate ways of assessing student performance.

PASS/FAIL, CREDIT/NO-CREDIT.   These, of course, are not truly grading systems; they do not sort students into categories or levels. Yet enough schools use Pass/Fail and Credit/No-credit systems that they deserve discussion. Indeed, we devoutly wish our own institutions would switch to this plan, which provides for evaluation of satisfactory work, yet does not have the negative effects of traditional grading plans. In P-F or Cr-NCr systems, the instructor simply establishes some basic aims and expectations for the course, what the student must achieve in order to pass or to receive credit. If the student completes the work, this is appropriately recorded on the course grade chart or on a transcript.

Some object to this kind of system on two grounds: First, they claim, it has no standards. Second, they say, it levels students, treating the good ones and the poorer ones the same. Both arguments, we think, can be rebutted by the writing teacher who has a good assessment program. If students are receiving a variety of forms of evaluation, standards clearly are in effect, even though they may not be described through letter grades. Indeed, it seems to us apparent that standards in a P-F, Cr-NCr system can actually be higher than in a conventional course where a "gentleman's 'C' " or a "damning 'D' " are still considered "passing" work. Further, though all students who *pass* under the P-F, Cr-NCr schemes receive the same grade, clearly the evaluation and response they receive in the course differ. If P-F, Cr-NCr systems fail to distinguish among students, it is only because the instructor did not evaluate students individually.

Unfortunately, despite their obvious advantages and their essential practicality and humaneness, P-F, Cr-NCr systems are diminishing, not growing in number. If you are lucky enough to teach in a system that uses one, rejoice. If you are not, lobby for a change. That failing, consider one of the alternatives that follow.

INDIVIDUAL PAPER GRADING. This is probably the most widely used grading plan and, to our mind, one of the least satisfactory. Placing grades on papers one at a time heightens awareness of grades and encourages students to engage in grade averaging—"I've got two 'C's and a 'B' already; there's no use trying for an 'A'." Students routinely ignore the teacher's carefully written comments and flip to the end of the paper where they find the all-important grade.

If grades must be given on individual papers, it seems terribly important that the criteria for excellence be carefully described in advance, so the students know what they need to do to achieve success. Too often individual paper grades seem to come as a complete surprise to the student, a sign that grades are blunting the ability of the student to evaluate his or her own work.

PORTFOLIO GRADING. Instead of grading individual papers, we recommend that the teacher consider grading a number of papers at a time through the student's portfolio. At selected intervals during the course, the student submits the portfolio, having spent time beforehand polishing papers into their best possible condition. The teacher then assesses the merits of the entire collection, or quite possibly, meets with the student in conference to discuss the evaluation.

Portfolio grading can still induce "grade consciousness," but it places emphasis on growth rather than solo performances. In commenting, the teacher can compare several compositions, discussing common strengths and weaknesses, focusing on needed areas of improvement, and so on. Because it allows students to revise over an extended period, the portfolio method more closely simulates the writing process than some other grading systems do.

As with individual paper grading, it is important for the instructor to make the criteria of evaluation explicit. There should be no mystery as to what is expected and how the portfolio will be graded. Often, in fact, the students can work with the teacher in developing criteria—an approach that ought to help students learn to become better judges of writing.

QUANTITY/QUALITY. This system, one we have used in both school and college writing classes, takes pressure off grades by making the letter grade a function of quantity of work (provided the quality is acceptable). For example, many teachers in the schools have experimented with *contract* grading, in which a student agrees to do a certain amount of work for a particular grade, with the criteria for various grades having been described by the teacher. If the student completes a contract, say, the writing of ten papers for a grade of "A," he or she automatically earns the grade. Quality control is maintained through other evaluation procedures, with the teacher making certain that papers are carefully prepared and revised, not just thrown together to satisfy the contract.

In a variation of that system, *point grading,* values are assigned to particular course activities. Writing a complete essay or story might carry ten points; maintaining a journal for the term might be worth twenty-five; submitting an article for the school newspaper might be valued at twenty. Appropriate grade ranges are established, and students are graded according to their accumulated totals, say, seventy points for a "C," eighty for a "B," and so on. In contrast to contracts, point grading is open ended; that is, the student can keep earning points to reach whatever level he or she can. Unfortunately, it also has the effect of making students "point hungry," so they may wind up writing solely to earn points instead of learning to write better.

A quantity plan we have found satisfactory is what we call *minimum plus.* We describe some basic, minimal requirements for the course, almost as one would for a Pass-Fail course. The students who complete the basic requirements, say, seven papers in a ten week term, are guaranteed a minimum grade, usually "B," provided the papers are of good quality. The "plus" levels involve additional work—more papers, longer papers, revised papers, submission of papers for publication, and so forth. Students are then free to work above the minimum levels as they wish.

THE LAST WORD—ON GRADING

Perhaps it is a measure of our concern about the effects of grading that we placed it as the very last item in this book. Grading complicates the efforts of the writing teacher and it interferes with his or her relationship with the students. One can minimize the effects on students through judicious choice of a grading system and by backing it up with a genuine assessment program. But we also suggest that in developing grading programs, the reader keep in mind the principle we have stressed throughout this book: People learn to write by writing and by getting a response to what they read. A grade, whether a bright and shining "A" or a "D" of despair, is no measure of a reader's response. The teacher owes it to the students to insure that no matter what the demands of the grading system, they receive honest, articulate, sympathetic responses to their writing.

APPENDIX A

WRITING CURRICULUM ARTIFACTS

Curriculum "artifacts" are the documents produced by teachers of writing: course syllabi and outlines, statements of goals, plans for individual lessons. Just as in anthropological and archaeological studies, one can use these artifacts to gain a sense of the people and the "culture" that created them. A curriculum artifact is a reflection of what happens inside a school or college classroom, though not a mirror image. All experienced teachers know that there is many a slip twixt designing a syllabus and actually implementing it in the classroom.

We present these artifacts with two aims in mind. First, we want to provide samples of what working teachers have prepared for their own use. These syllabi and curriculum outlines give the reader a sense of how teachers go about putting their ideas into practice. Second, we recognize that no book can fully summarize or characterize what happens inside a composition classroom. We think these curriculum artifacts will help to fill in the gap between our text and actual teaching practice.

OVERVIEW OF ENGLISH 102, COLLEGE WRITING I

FINDLAY COLLEGE*
Findlay, Ohio

This outline was prepared as a model for use by the English Department of Findlay College in conducting its required first year writing course. It provides a sound and thoughtful set of goals and makes clear the general teaching strategies for the course. The general plan of the course combines an emphasis on teaching writing as process with a flow of course content from personal experiences to public writing and more formal kinds of persuasion. Rhetorical discussions are incorporated naturally into the assignments, as are comments on mechanical and syntactic correctness. With its concluding focus on research, it obviously is intended to satisfy the service function of a college writing course—preparing students to write in other courses—but there is no abrupt break between personal and public writing.

---

1. OBJECTIVES

In English 102, students should:

a. Gain knowledge of, and experience using, a reliable writing process.
b. Gain initital experience writing for several different audiences.
c. Gain initial experience with forms of writing that promote the formulation of judgments about personal experience and the development of analytical and critical-thinking abilities.
d. Gain confidence drawing insights and supporting details from personal experience and from written sources.
e. Be able to utilize a, b, c, and d to create written products characterized by effective unity, organization, and support; by adequate (though not necessarily sophisticated) word choices; and by usage and mechanics that conform to Edited American English.
f. Gain knowledge of the qualities of effective writing above and be able to use it to improve writing by conscious revision.
g. Gain initial experience collaborating with other students toward mutual improvement of writing.

---

* This document was sent to us by Richard Gebhardt, Writing Director, and it is reprinted by permission.

2.   GENERAL STRATEGY

English 102 will focus on writing process. It will introduce students to the "stages" of generating, drafting, and revising. It will, especially, emphasize the generation of ideas and details and the drafting of papers—and the ways that these interrelate with concern for audience and the form of writing. (For example, students might learn how to generate ideas for personal writing, how to draft personal material for a non-intimate audience, how to generate an analytic paper for an audience of college students, how to use critical reading strategies to get started on a summary or locate evidence for an argument, etc.)

This intertwined concern for process, audience, and form suggests that the course will work in a "spiral" method, with students returning, at several points, to the matter of process as new forms or audiences are brought into the course.

The course will begin with an emphasis on personal writing (in which the students can consider matters of process and audience without having to cope with abstract subject matter); fairly soon, however, the course will turn to more analytic forms of writing.

Behind the course stands the assumption that writing is a key element in a person's education, as well as a useful career skill. Course orientation and materials—and staff attitude—should suggest that writing is, perhaps, the most important thing students will learn in college—a view supported by the fact that English 102 is the only course required of all Findlay students.

3.   GENERAL SCHEDULE OF ENGLISH 102, COLLEGE WRITING I

INTRODUCTIONS

Wk. 1   Diagnostic writings, readings.
        Content: The role of writing in your education and future career.
        Overview of forms of writing to be used later.

PERSONAL WRITING

Wk. 2   Narration   Interspersed through unit:
   3   Describing places, peo-   Methods of generating and draft-

ple, that occur in the narration. (In-class Writing A)	ing for audience on a personal topic.
4 Forming judgments about the significance of your experiences. (Generalizing from details)	Analytic reading of biolgraphical and personal-essay material. Fairly many short assignments, quick feedback coming from students as well as teacher. Introduction to collaborative work.

5-6   Key Paper 1:
Personal essay using narration, description, and judgments about the meaning of personal experiences. The two-week unit begins, again, with work on generation and audience for the paper. Draft complete for student commentary by Monday. 500–1000 words.

ANALYTICAL WRITING

Wk. 7	Summarizing and drawing conclusions from written sources.	Work on process and with analytic reading continues through this unit.
8	Locating propaganda, faulty logic, and undersupported generalizations in articles by others.	Work on methods of inductive thought. Short assignments, quick feedback.
9	Comparing/contrasting ideas found in written sources with each other and with your own views. (In-class Writing B)	More group work than in Personal Unit.
10	Avoiding logical problems and underdevelopment in your statements.	

11   Key Paper 2:
Builds on the reading and short writings of 7–10. Topic: Form a judgment about a subject on the basis of written materials. Work from several articles, etc. on a subject. Write a paper that clarifies the issues, helps the reader through contradictions in the sources, presents the student's conclusions. 750–1500 words.

PERSUASIVE WRITING

12 Generating for purposes of argumentation, persuasion.
Finding topics.
Finding personal views.
Reading and other research.
(In-class Writing C)

13 Library work and summarizing, forming conclusions about things read. Forming trial thesis statements.

Locating "clash" with writers in research.
Note taking.

14-15 Key Paper 3: Convince an audience that your judgments are accurate on a topic on which there is a range of available opinion. Begin with drafting for this sort of paper; emphasize audience as a guide in drafting. Include stuff on expanding a thesis with logic and evidence. 1000–2000 words.

SYLLABUS FOR ENGLISH 840, "WRITING WORKSHOP FOR TEACHERS"

MICHIGAN STATE UNIVERSITY
East Lansing, Michigan

This course was designed by Stephen Judy for experienced teachers; thus it combines actual writing with discussion of teaching techniques. The course was split into two strands, "Course A" and "Course B," corresponding to the two major course components. Course A shows our "experience-based" approach to writing, beginning with personal writing and leading to exploration and research. Course B, the pedagogy course, begins with basic issues, moves into a step-by-step discussion of the writing process, and concludes with individualized workshops on specific teaching problems.

TEXTS

James E. Miller, Jr. WORD, SELF, REALITY. Dodd, Mead, 1972.

Peter Elbow. WRITING WITHOUT TEACHERS. Oxford, 1974.

National Council of Teachers of English. ENGLISH JOURNAL. November, 1974, "Teaching Writing"

(Recommended resource) Rosellen Brown and others. THE WHOLE WORD CATALOGUE. Virgil Books/Teachers and Writers Collaborative, 1972.

COURSE OBJECTIVES AND REQUIREMENTS

COMPONENT "A" (Mondays). This part of the course is designed to help you extend your writing skills and increase your sensitivity to the nature of the writing process by engaging in a variety of writing activities. On (most) Mondays you will be asked to bring six copies (ditto, mimeo, carbon, or photocopy) of the second draft of something you have written. Suggestions for writing will be distributed in class. Papers will be discussed in small groups in the manner of Peter Elbow's "teacherless" writing class. Two of the pieces you write will be further refined, polished, and edited for publication in a class anthology. (Due dates: May 2, June 1) Background readings in the Miller book will form the basis for discussion on Mondays.

COMPONENT "B" (Wednesdays). In this segment, we will look directly at practical teaching techniques for elementary, secondary, and college writing programs. The earliest sessions (April) will focus on basic issues and problems in writing instruction: Why write? Why can't Johnny and Jane write? What is the writing process? How can it be taught? Later meetings (May) will focus on specific strategies and will include "make 'n take" materials preparation sessions. Readings in Elbow and the November 1976 EJ will be required. A supplementary reading list will be supplied with books on reserve in the English Department Library.

GRADING POLICY

For a grade of 3.0. Complete all assigned reading and writing satisfactorily; attend and participate in most class meetings.

For a grade of 3.5 or 4.0. Demonstrate excellence in one or two of the following three areas:

1. Monday writings (overall quality, individual improvement, range and diversity of writing)
2. Class participation (willingness to contribute to discussions, energy invested in making large and small group discussions work)
3. Individual and supplementary reading. (Opportunities for free reading will be given during May. Keep an informal log of your reading.)

Course "A" (Mondays)

APRIL 4

"The Writing Process: Getting Started"

Writing: Interest inventories, and freewriting

Reading: Elbow, "Freewriting Exercises" (3–10); Miller, Intro. and I, "Language as Creation" (1–41)

Course "B" (Wednesdays)

APRIL 6

"Why Can't Johnny Write?"

Reading: November '76 EJ, articles by Burton (5–6), Weingartner (12–14), and the "Close-up," pp. 29–46 (articles by Elgin, Bergen, Fox, Stoen, and Parker/Meskin)

APRIL 11

"The Creation of Self"

Writing: Reminiscence, memoir
Reading: Miller, II, "Writing, Thinking, Feeling" (42−72)

APRIL 18

"Who I Am; or, Who You Think I Am"

Writing: Personal essays, narratives
Reading: Miller, III, "Language and Meaning": (73−106)

APRIL 25

"Who I Am;
The Me Nobody Knows"

Writing: Dreams, Visions, Fantasies
Reading: Miller, IV, "Writing as Discovery: Inner Worlds"

MAY 2

Writing: From your writing to date, select one piece and revise it for publication in the class anthology. Bring multiple copies to class.

Discussion and planning for remainder of term.

MAY 9

"Interweaving the World"

APRIL 13

"What We Do/Don't Know About Teaching Writing"

Reading: Nov. EJ, article by Blake, pp. 49−55. Highly recommended: "The State of Knowledge About Composition," in Research in Written Composition (NCTE, 1963), pp. 29−53. (On reserve)

APRIL 20

"The Writing Process: Planning, Drafting, Cooking, etc."

Reading: Judy, "On Clock Watching and Composing" (mimeo); Elbow, Chaps. 2,3, "Cooking," "Growing" (12−75)

APRIL 27

"The Writing Process: Revising, Editing, Publishing"

Reading: Koch, "Writer and Audience" (mimeo); Judy, "Writing for the Here and Now" (mimeo); Elbow, Chaps, 4, 5, "Teacherless Writing" (76−146)

MAY 4, 11, 18, 25

At this point course "B" will become a series of small group workshops on specialized topics in teaching writing. Background readings will be on reserve. Sample topics:

Teaching creative writing
Personal writing
Media composition
Drama and writing

Writing: Papers of analysis and synthesis
Reading: Miller, V, "Writing as Exploration"

MAY 16

"Exploring/Researching/Probing"

Writing: Investigative paper
Reading: Miller and Judy, "Exploring/Researching/Probing" (mimeo)

MAY 25

"Causes and Commitments"

Writing: Persuasion
Reading: Miller, VI, "The Individual Voice"

MAY 30

Writing: Second polished writing due in multiple copies.

Improvisation and writing
Oral composing
College prep writing
Brass tacks writing
Writing for the junior high
Tutoring centers
Grammar and spelling
Evaluating writing
Sentence-combining
Students as editors
Composition and career education
The classroom structure
Publishing writing
Writing contests

JUNE 1

"Dear Abby Fidditch"

Everything you always wanted to know about writing but had nobody to ask.

BASIC ASSUMPTIONS ABOUT THE DEVELOPMENT OF WRITING SKILLS

SAN DIEGO CITY SCHOOLS*
San Diego, California

This curriculum artifact is the work of three San Diego teachers, Mary A. Barr, Carolyn Carey, and Loyal Carlon, working in consultation with other faculty members. It is an excellent statement of assumptions about teaching writing, a statement of philosophy of the kind we think every school or college faculty ought to develop. It deals with broad, general goals for writing as well as such traditional problems of handling correctness.

The teachers represented in this collection of teaching strategies have developed approaches to writing stemming from the following assumptions. You will note that all assumptions deal with the entire process of writing and focus on the student and his needs.

1. Every writing assignment must be directed to a specific audience, preferably one that is significant to the writer.

2. Students need to learn to write for a variety of audiences.

3. Not all student writing needs to be or should be graded, but most of it needs to be published—for parents, peers, and others significant in the students' lives.

4. Effective writing instruction provides frequent and immediate response to the writer by competent and respected readers. The ratio of writer to reader must be low enough to facilitate this process. (The recommendation of a 25−1 student−teacher ratio by San Diego City Schools English teachers, the California Association of Teachers of English and the National Council of Teachers of English is pertinent here.)

5. The student will gain greater facility in written communication only as he/she sees it as an essential part of the total thinking process. Frequent writing practice itself does not necessarily improve writing skill.

* Submitted by Jesse Perry and Patricia Phelan. Reprinted by permission.

6. Composition skill requires the ability to conceptualize; this ability is frequently strengthened and motivated in oral discussion.
7. The mechanics of written composition—punctuation, capitalization, spelling, etc.—must be seen in the proper perspective, as supportive of meaning and purpose. Correcting dummy sentences in textbooks or memorizing the spellings or meanings of words not used in context will not improve student writing.
8. Writing skill involves much more than is measured by standardized tests, which tend to deal with superficial aspects of English usage.
9. Writing skill should have its own reason for being at the time it is used, rather than just being a response to the "this-will-be-good-for-you-later" syndrome.
10. The English classroom should be equipped for writing instruction. Equipment should include tables (to allow ample room to work and to encourage oral exchange), typewriters, cassette recorders and a ditto machine or copier.
11. James Moffett is right: "More learning takes place when students of different ability, achievement, socioeconomic class, dialect, sex and race are mixed together. The English classroom should be as richly varied a speech community as can be mustered."* The 1975 ENGLISH LANGUAGE FRAMEWORK FOR CALIFORNIA PUBLIC SCHOOLS also. speaks of the restrictiveness of rigid patterns of 'grouping' which limit the linguistic environment in which boys and girls learn English and which tend to inhibit language development."†
12. Course content, including that in electives, must serve as a vehicle for learning the basic skills in speaking, listening, reading and writing.
13. Classroom environment must demonstrate that the thoughts, needs and learning modes of each student are important.
14. A major goal of English instruction is the flexible use of dialect appropriate to the needs of the speaker. The English classroom is a good place to explore the diversity of language, thereby enlarging options.
15. Because learning to write is a process, class time should be devoted to prewriting, writing, evaluating and revising activities.

* James Moffett, *A Student-Centered Language Arts Curriculum, Grades K-13: A Handbook for Teachers* (New York: Houghton Mifflin, 1973), p. 5.
† p. vii.

WORKING DOCUMENT: GRADES 7–8, LANGUAGE ARTS

BENTON COMMUNITY JUNIOR HIGH SCHOOL*
Newhall, Iowa

A great many junior and senior high school faculties across the country are faced with the assignment of "accountability"—showing that their programs are producing results. Too often these programs degenerate into listing of minimal skills objectives, with testing limited to parts-of-speech, spelling, mechanics, and so on. This document, prepared by Mike Crum and Melvin Thrusby with the help of the Benton Community J.H.S. faculty, shows an alternative. First, the goals of the language arts program are explained, and these goals include humanistic goals, not just skill objectives. Then the faculty explains how it will measure growth in writing. Note that they are concerned with observing mastery of the stages of the writing process and they use a mix of actual writing samples and formal and standardized tests. Too, they are as concerned about success in personal, expressive writing as with more formal kinds of public writing.

PHILOSOPHY
Language arts is a student oriented program in which students explore the interactive processes of composing and comprehending. The process of composing consists of writing, speaking, and visual expression. The process of comprehending consists of reading, listening, and observing. The exploration of these language processes will improve the students' self-concept and create an awareness of how human needs are satisfied through communication.

PROGRAM LEVEL OBJECTIVES—WRITING

1. Students at all program levels will demonstrate growth in their ability to control the process of writing. The process of writing is defined as a series of steps used to generate a piece of written

---

* Submitted by James Davis, Grant Wood Educational Agency, Cedar Rapids, Iowa. Reprinted by permission.

communication. These steps consist of pre-drafting, drafting, re-drafting, and post-drafting. The different steps in the writing process will be measured on a pre and post basis by a combination of writing samples, attitude surveys, and criterion referenced tests.

2. Students at all program levels will grow in their knowledge of the importance attached to writing skills. An attitude survey on a pre and post basis will be used to determine growth.

3. Students at all program levels will demonstrate growth in their ability to produce written communication that reveals personal feelings and ideas. Items from the National Assessment of Educational Progress on a pre and post basis will be used to determine growth.

4. Students in the 7th grade developmental program, in the 7th grade accelerated program, and in all 8th grade programs will demonstrate growth in their ability to produce written communication that informs a reader. Items from the National Assessment of Educational Progress on a pre and post basis will be used to determine growth.

5. Students in the 7th grade accelerated program, in the 8th grade accelerated program and in the 8th grade developmental program will demonstrate a growth in their ability to produce written communication that persuades a reasonable audience. Items from the National Assessment of Educational Progress on a pre and post basis will be used to determine growth.

APPENDIX B

CONTESTS AND PLACES TO PUBLISH WRITING

Writing contests offer students a way of writing for audiences outside their immediate experience. Sometimes the teacher will find contests at the college or on the state level. *The Writer* magazine is an excellent source of information about current writing contests, including those open to students. Another useful resource is *Gadney's Guide to Contests and Awards* (1979). From time to time education related journals such as *The English Journal, Language Arts, Media & Methods,* and *Teachers and Writers Magazine* will announce contests and awards. Among the national contests that have a reasonably good and long history are the following*:

ATLANTIC MONTHLY Creative Writing Contest (8 Arlington Street, Boston, Massachusetts 02116).

GUIDEPOSTS MAGAZINE Youth Writing Contest (747 Third Avenue, New York, New York 10017).

National Council of Teachers of English Achievement in Writing Program (1111 Kenyon Road, Urbana, Illinois 61801).

Scholastic Magazines Creative Writing Awards (50 West 44th Street, New York, New York 10036).

SEVENTEEN MAGAZINE Short Story Contest (320 Park Avenue, New York, New York 10022).

National magazines that either solicit articles by young people or accept articles that deal with young persons' interests include the following† (Examine the publication statements inside a current issue of the magazine or check the latest copy of *Literary Market Place* or *Writer's Handbook* for the most recent policy statements.):

AMERICAN GIRL (830 Third Avenue, New York, New York 10022).

BOYS' LIFE (North Brunswick, New Jersey 08902).

---

* *Source:* John Bennett, "A Directory of Writing Contests," *The English Journal,* 64(January 1975), 98–100.

† *Source:* A. S. Burack, editor, *The Writer's Handbook* (Boston: The Writer, Inc., 1980).

CO-ED (Scholastic Magazines, Inc., 50 West 44th Street, New York, New York 10036).

GRIT (Williamsport, Pennsylvania 17701).

KEYNOTER (101 East Erie Street, Chicago, Illinois 60611).

LISTEN MAGAZINE (6830 Laurel Street, N.W., Washington, D.C. 20012).

SCHOLASTIC SCOPE (Scholastic Magazines, Inc., 50 West 44th Street, New York, New York 10036).

SEVENTEEN (850 Third Avenue, New York, New York 10022).

TEEN MAGAZINE (8490 Sunset Boulevard, Los Angeles, California 90069).

YOUNG ATHLETE (1601 114th Street, S.E., Bellevue, Washington 98004).

APPENDIX C

COMPOSITION JOURNALS AND PROFESSIONAL ORGANIZATIONS

The following list of journals and organizations is intended to provide an introduction to the principal professional resources available to the writing teacher. In addition, a great many publications not listed here carry articles on composition, as a check of *Education Index* will reveal. Writing teachers should know, too, that many of the national organizations listed here have state and local affiliates that meet regularly and often publish journals and newsletters of their own.

CEA Critic, CEA Forum. Both published by the College English Association (see separate entry). The *Critic* presents longer articles with an emphasis on theory; the *Forum* is concerned with day-to-day teaching problems. Both publications regularly include articles on composition.

College English. Published by the National Council of Teachers of English (see separate entry). This journal, published eight times a year, is a major source of information for practicing college teachers. Focus issues on composition are published regularly.

College English Association. Holds annual meeting in the spring of the year and is concerned with theory and practice of teaching college literature, language, and composition. (Department of English, Texas A & M University, College Station, Texas 77843).

Conference on College Composition and Communication. Holds annual meeting in the spring of the year. Publishes *College Composition and Communication*, an excellent quarterly journal that is of interest to secondary as well as college teachers. Membership is obtained through the National Council of Teachers of English (see separate entry).

Conference on English Education. An organization of those who prepare English teachers and of public school language arts administrators. Publishes *English Education*, a quarterly that often presents articles on teaching writing or training teachers to teach writing. Holds an annual meeting in the spring of the year. Membership is obtained through the National Council of Teachers of English (see separate entry).

Composition and Teaching. An annual publication of San Jose State University and Goucher College, with an emphasis on practical classroom applications. (Goucher College, Towson, Maryland 21204).*

The English Journal. Published eight times each year for junior and senior high school English teachers. Frequently includes articles or devotes whole issues to composition. Subscriptions obtained through membership in the National Council of Teachers of English (see separate entry).

Fforum. Quarterly newsletter of the English Composition Board of the University of Michigan, which encapsulates composition theory for practitioners. (1025 Angell Hall, Ann Arbor, Michigan 48109).

Freshman English News. Composition oriented journal for freshman English teachers, published three times each year. (Department of English, Texas Christian University, Fort Worth, Texas 76129).*

Freshman English Notes. Quarterly newsletter with a focus on college teaching. (Department of English, University of Nevada, Las Vegas, Nevada 89154).*

Journal of Basic Writing. Semiannual journal devoted to teaching underprepared college students. (City University of New York, Instructional Resource Center, 535 East 80th Street, New York, New York 10021).*

Language Arts. Eight issues each year for elementary school teachers. Frequently publishes articles on writing. Subscription comes with membership in the National Council of Teachers of English (see separate entry).

Media & Methods. Published nine times each year, this commercial publication frequently presents articles teaching writing. Despite its title, it is concerned with much more than media education. (401 N. Broad Street, Philadelphia, Pennsylvania 19108).

National Council of Teachers of English. Publishes *College English*, *English Journal*, *Language Arts*, *Research in the Teaching of English*, *English Education*, and *College Composition and Communication*. Membership in

* Source: William Woods, Tina Bennett, Michael Forinash, Barbara Smith, Edward Stucky, and Helen Throckmorton, "A Guide to Publishing Opportunities for Teachers of Writing, "*The English Journal*, 69(January 1980), 97–100.

the Council includes a subscription to one of the first three journals. Additional journals may be purchased. Institutional and library memberships are possible. NCTE holds its annual meeting in the fall of the year, providing a major forum for writing teachers. In addition, it sponsors numerous spring workshops and conferences. (1111 Kenyon Road, Urbana, Illinois 61801).

Philosophy and Rhetoric. A quarterly, refereed journal with a strong philosophical bent. Little practical information. (240 Sparks Building, University Park, Pennsylvania 16802).*

Research on the Teaching of English. Quarterly journal presenting many research studies on writing. Published by the National Council of Teachers of English (see separate entry).

Rhetoric Society Quarterly. A heavily theoretical journal specifically disavowing interest in classroom applications. (Department of Philosophy, St. Cloud State University, St. Cloud, Minnesota 56301).*

Teachers & Writers Magazine. An outstanding practical magazine, published three times a year, with an emphasis on creative writing techniques for the upper elementary school grades. (84 Fifth Avenue, New York, New York 10011).

WLA Newsletter. WLA stands for "Writing as a Liberating Activity." This occasional newsletter is of interest to theoreticians and practitioners alike, both school and college writing teachers. (Department of English, Findlay College, Findlay, Ohio 45840).

BIBLIOGRAPHY

Adams, Charles, Edwin L. Godkin, and Josiah Quincy. "Report of the Committee on Composition and Rhetoric." *Reports of the Visiting Committees of the Board of Overseers of Harvard College from February 6, 1890 to January 8, 1902, Inclusive.* Cambridge, Mass.: Harvard University, 1902.

Amberg, John. "Among the Pork and Beans." *The English Journal,* 66(December 1977), 37–40.

Bain, Alexander. *English Composition and Rhetoric.* New York: D. Appleton, 1869.

Baur, Pamela, Marge O'Connor, Mary Sniegowski, Linda Webber, and Jane Wibirt. "The Me Tree." Unpublished paper. Central Michigan University, 1979.

Beck, James P. "Theory and Practice of Interdisciplinary English." *The English Journal,* 69(February 1980), 28–32.

Breakey, Susan. "A Strategy for Beginning a Complementary Program for Language Arts and Visual Arts." Unpublished paper. Michigan State University, 1980.

Britton, James, Tony Burgess, Nancy Martin, Alex McCloud, and Harold Rosen. *The Development of Writing Abilities, 11–18.* London: Macmillan Education, 1975.

Brostoff, Anita and Lois Josephs Fowler. "The Right Questions." Unpublished paper. Carnegie-Mellon University, 1979.

Bruner, Ingrid, J. C. Mathes, and Dwight Stevenson. *The Technician as Writer.* Indianapolis: Bobbs Merrill, 1980.

Bruner, Jerome. *The Process of Education.* New York: Vintage, 1960.

Carnicelli, Thomas. "The Writing Conference: A One-to-One Conversation." In Timothy R. Donovan and Ben W. McClelland, eds. *Eight Approaches to Teaching Composition.* Urbana, Ill.: National Council of Teachers of English, 1980.

Carter, John Marshall. "Publish or Perish: Writing Inspiration and Reward." *The English Journal,* 68(October 1979), 53–55.

Chomsky, Noam. *Syntactic Structures.* The Hague: Mouton & Company, 1964.

Christensen, Francis. *Notes Toward a New Rhetoric.* New York: Harper & Row, 1967.

———and Bonnijean Christensen. *A New Rhetoric.* New York: Harper & Row, 1976.

Clark, Christopher. Discussion with the Teacher Education Committee, Department of English, Michigan State University, April 1980.

College Entrance Examination Board. *On Further Examination: Report of the Advisory Panel on the Scholastic Aptitude Test Decline.* New York: CEEB, 1977.

Conference on College Composition and Communication. "The Students' 'Right' to Their Own Language." *College Composition and Communication* (Fall 1974).

Cooper, Charles R. and Lee Odell. *Evaluating Writing.* Urbana, Ill.: National Council of Teachers of English, 1977.

Corbett, Edward P. J. *Classical Rhetoric for the Modern Student.* New York: Oxford University Press, 1971.

Cowan, Gregory and Elizabeth Cowan. *Writing.* New York: John Wiley & Sons, 1980.

Crews, Frederick. *The Random House Handbook.* 2nd edition. New York: Random House, 1977.

Dewey, John. *Experience and Education*. New York: Macmillan, 1938.

Diederich, Paul. *Measuring Growth in English*. Urbana, Ill: National Council of Teachers of English, 1974.

Dixon, John. *Growth Through English*. London, New York, and Champaign, Ill.: The National Association for the Teaching of English, the Modern Language Association, and the National Council of Teachers of English, 1967. (Third edition, 1975).

Douglas, Wallace. "On Teaching the Process of Writing." In Alexander Frazier, ed., *New Directions in Elementary English*. Urbana, Ill.: National Council of Teachers of English, 1966a. And in the same collection, "The Place of Rhetoric in the Preparation of Composition Teachers." 1966b.

―――. "Some Basic Processes in Composition." Evanston, Ill.: Curriculum Center in English, Northwestern University, 1963.

Duke, Charles F. "The Student-Centered Conference and the Writing Process." *The English Journal*, 64(December 1975), 44−47.

Elbow, Peter. "Teaching Writing While Teaching Something Else." *Fforum*, 1(Fall 1979), 4−7, 14.

―――. *Writing Without Teachers*. New York: Oxford University Press, 1973.

Emig, Janet. *The Composing Process of Twelfth Graders*. Urbana, Ill.: National Council of Teachers of English, 1971.

―――― and Robert P. Parker, Jr. "Responding to Student Writing: Building a Theory of the Evaluating Process." New Brunswick: Rutgers University, 1976. ERIC ED 136−257.

Fadiman, Clifton and James Howard. *Empty Pages: A Search for Writing Competence in School and Society*. Belmont, Calif.: Fearon Pitman Publishers, 1979.

Felton, Bruce and Mark Fowler. "Our 60th Anniversary Salute to 60 Years of the Best, the Worst, the Wackiest in American Writing." *Writer's Digest* (January 1980), 23−35.

Flesch, Rudolf. *Look It Up: A Deskbook of American Spelling and Style*. New York: Harper & Row, 1977.

―――. *Why Johnny Can't Read and What You Can Do About It*. New York: Harper & Row, 1966.

Fox, Patricia. "Why Johnny Can't and the Cat in the Hat." *The English Journal*, 65(November 1976), 38−39.

Gebhardt, Richard. "Imagination and Discipline in the Composition Class." *The English Journal*, 66(December 1977), 26−32.

Gibson, Walker. *Persona: A Style Study for Readers and Writers*. New York: Random House, 1969.

Gillis, Candida. "The English Classroom 1977." *The English Journal*, 66(September 1977), 20−26.

Graves, Robert and Alan Hodge. *The Reader Over Your Shoulder*. London: Jonathan Cape, 1943.

Greenberg, Arthur. "City As School." *The English Journal*, 65(October 1976), 60−62.

Hagemann, Meyly Chin. "Taking the Wrench Out of Letter Writing." *The English Journal*, 69(April 1980), 38−39.

Hawley, Robert C., Sidney B. Simon, and D. D. Britton. *Composition for Personal Growth*. New York: Hart, 1973.

Haynes, Elizabeth. "Using Research in Preparing to Teach Writing." *The English Journal*, 67(January 1978), 82−88.

Heck, Shirley F. "Planning: The Key to Successful Interdisciplinary Teaching." *Kappa Delta Pi Record* (April 1979), 116−121.

Herndon, Edward. *How to Survive in Your Native Land.* New York: Simon & Schuster, 1971.

Herum, John and D. W. Cummings. *Writing: Plans, Drafts, & Revisions.* New York: Random House, 1971.

Hilson, Linda Rae and Melinda G. Kramer. *The Right Book.* Englewood Cliffs, N.J.: Prentice-Hall, 1980.

Hoffman, Eleanor and John Schifsky. "Designing Writing Assignments." *The English Journal*, 66(December 1977), 41−45.

Holt, John. *How Children Fail.* New York: Pittman, 1964.

Jacobs, Suzanne. Letter to the editor. *The English Journal*, 63(October 1974).

Judy, Stephen. "On Clock Watching and Composing." *The English Journal*, 57(March 1968), 360−366.

——— and Susan J. Judy. *Gifts of Writing.* New York: Charles Scribner's Sons, 1980.

Kelly, Lou. *From Dialogue to Discourse: An Open Approach to Competence and Creativity.* Glenview, Ill.: Scott, Foresman and Company, 1972.

Kitzhaber, Albert Raymond. *Rhetoric in American Colleges, 1850−1900.* Unpublished doctoral dissertation. University of Washington, 1953.

Koch, Carl and James M. Brazil. *Strategies for Teaching the Composing Process.* Urbana, Ill.: National Council of Teachers of English, 1968.

Kohl, Herbert. *36 Children.* New York: Signet, 1967.

Kozol, Jonathan. *Death at an Early Age.* Boston: Houghton Mifflin, 1967.

Ledbetter, J. T. "Just Think." *The English Journal*, 63(September 1974), 50−52.

Levinger, Larry. "The Human Side of Illiteracy." *The English Journal*, 67(November 1978), 28−32.

Lewis, William. "Two Technical Writing Assignments." *The English Journal*, 67(April 1978), 65−68.

Luban, Nina, Ann Matsuhashi, and Tom Reigstad. "One-to-One to Write: Establishing an Individual Conference Writing Place." *The English Journal*, 67(November 1978), 30−35.

Mack, Karin and Eric Skjei. *Overcoming Writing Blocks.* Los Angeles: J. P. Tarcher, 1979.

Macrorie, Ken. *Uptaught.* Rochelle Park, N. J.: Hayden Books, 1970.

Marzano, Robert. "The Sentence Combining Myth." *The English Journal*, 65(February 1976), 57−59.

Mathes, J. C., Dwight W. Stevenson, and Peter Klaver. "Technical Writing: The Engineering Educator's Responsibility." *CEA Forum*, 10(December 1979), 1−5. Originally appeared in *Engineering Education.*

Maxwell, John C. "National Assessment of Writing: Useless and Uninteresting?" *The English Journal*, 62(December 1973), 1254−1257.

McAndrew, Donald. "Measuring Growth in an Interdisciplinary Humanities Course." *The English Journal*, 69(February 1980), 52−56.

Mellon, John. *Transformational Sentence-Combining*. Urbana, Ill.: National Council of Teachers of English, 1969.

Miller, James E., Jr. *Word, Self, Reality*. New York: Dodd, Mead, 1972.

—— and Stephen N. Judy. *Writing in Reality*. New York: Harper & Row, 1978.

Miller, Susan. *Writing: Process and Product*. Cambridge, Mass.: Winthrop Publishers, 1976.

Moffett, James. *Teaching the Universe of Discourse*. Boston: Houghton Mifflin, 1968.

Moore, Joseph B. "A Writing Week." *The English Journal*, 67(November 1978), 39–41.

Morgan, Fred. *Here and Now III*. New York: Harcourt Brace Jovanovich, 1979.

Murray, Donald M. "Teach the Motivating Force of Revision," *The English Journal*, 67(October 1978), 56–60.

——. "Writing as Process: How Writing Finds Its Own Meaning." In Timothy R. Donovan and Ben W. McClelland, eds. *Eight Approaches to Teaching Composition*. Urbana, Ill.: National Council of Teachers of English, 1980.

Murray, Lindley. *English Grammar, Adapted to the Different Classes of Learners*. York, England: Longman, Rees, Orme, Brown, Green, and Longman, 1795.

Nairn, Allan and Ralph Nader. *The Reign of ETS: The Corporation that Makes Up Minds*. Published privately by Ralph Nader. Washington, D.C., 1980.

National Council of Teachers of English. *The National Interest and the Teaching of English*. Champaign, Ill.: NCTE, 1961.

National Education Association. Report of the Committee on Secondary School Studies. Washington, D.C.: Government Printing Office, 1893.

The National Writing Project Newsletter. Berkeley, Calif.: University of California School of Education, 1978.

Newman, Edwin. *A Civil Tongue*. Indianapolis: Bobbs Merrill, 1976.

——. *Strictly Speaking*. Indianapolis: Bobbs Merrill, 1974.

Newsweek. "Why Johnny Can't Write" (December 8, 1975).

O'Hare, Frank. *Sentence Combining*. Urbana, Ill.: National Council of Teachers of English, 1973.

Ontario Ministry of Education. "Evaluation of Learning Environments." In *Language Across the Curriculum*. Ontario: Ontario Ministry of Education, 1978, 18.

Raymond, James. *Writing (Is an Unnatural Act)*. New York: Harper & Row, 1980.

Reid, Richard. "Ideographs as Cultural Documents." In Stephen Botein et al., compilers, *Experiments in History Teaching*. Cambridge, Mass.: Danforth Foundation, 1977, 23.

Roberts, Paul. *The Roberts English Series*. New York: Harcourt Brace, and World, 1967.

——. *Understanding English*. New York: Harper Brothers, 1958.

Rosen, Lois. Dissertation in progress. Michigan State University, 1980.

Rosenblatt, Louise. *Literature as Exploration*. New York: D. Appleton, 1938.

——. *The Reader, the Text, and the Poem*. Carbondale, Ill.: Southern Illinois University Press, 1979.

Ross, Frederick and Mitchell Jarosz. "Integrating Science Writing: A Biology Instructor and an English Teacher Get Together." *The English Journal*. 67(April 1978), 51–55.

Rout, Kay. "Their Master's Voice." *Good Writing,* 4(Winter 1980), 1.

Ruchlis, Hy and Belle Sharefkin. *Reality Centered Learning.* New York: Citation, 1975.

Scholastic American Literature Program. New York: Scholastic Book Services, 1977.

Sledd, James. *A Short Introduction to English Grammar.* Chicago: Scott, Foresman, 1959.

Snow, Mary. *Arts in Education Evaluation.* Pennsylvania Department of Education, 1979.

Spikol, Art. "Follow My Lead." *Writer's Digest,* 60(April 1980), 8 – 9.

Squire, James R. and Roger K. Applebee. *High School English Instruction Today.* New York: Appleton-Century-Crofts, 1968.

Stilgove, John R. "Landscape History." In Stephen Botein, et al., compilers, *Experiments in History Teaching.* Cambridge, Mass.: Danforth Foundation, 1967.

Strong, William. "Back to Basics and Beyond." *The English Journal,* 65(February 1976), 56, 60 – 64.

Styles, Ken and Gray Cavanagh. "Language Across the Curriculum: The Art of Questioning and Responding." *The English Journal,* 69(February 1980), 24 – 27.

Suhor, Charles. *Mass Testing in Composition: Is It Worth Doing Badly?* New Orleans Public Schools, 1977.

Talbott, Frank. "Creative Writing in the Elementary Class." *The English Leaflet.* 74(Winter 1980), 9 – 13.

Tate, Gary, Chair. "Standards for Basic Skills Writing Programs." The Report of the Committee on Writing Standards. Urbana, Ill.: National Council of Teachers of English, 1979.

Thurber, Samuel. "An Address to English Teachers." *Education,* 18(1898), 515 – 526.

Tierney, Gilbert and Stephen Judy. "The Assignment Makers." *The English Journal,* 61(February 1972), 265 – 269.

Walshe, R. D. "What's Basic to Teaching Writing." *The English Journal,* 68(December 1979), 51 – 56.

Watkins, Floyd C. and Karl F. Knight. *Writer to Writer: Readings on the Craft of Writing.* Boston: Houghton Mifflin, 1966.

Wilkes, John. "Science Writing: Who? What? How? *The English Journal,* 67(April 1978), 56 – 60.

Woods, William F. et al. "A Directory of Publishing Opportunities for Teachers of Writing." *The English Journal,* 69(January 1980), 97 – 100.

Zavatsky, Bill and Ron Padgett. *The Whole Word Catalogue II.* New York: McGraw-Hill, 1975.

Zimmerman, Marvin. "The Creative Writing Class: Writers in Search of an Audience." *The English Journal,* 68(October 1979), 51 – 52.

INDEX